◯ CONTENTS

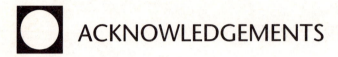 ACKNOWLEDGEMENTS

Many people gave us assistance of various kinds while writing this book. In particular, we would like to thank Professor David Bridges for permission to quote from Bridges, D., Elliott, J. and McKee, A. (1995) *Competence Based Higher Education and the Standards Methodology: Final Report*, Margaret Handy for essential word-processing help, David Howe and Phil Leather, Phil Moore, Professor John Tomlinson, Chris Husbands, Linda Evans and Ian Abbott.

 **INTRODUCTION**

Ten years ago, mentoring was almost unheard of in the context of initial teacher education (ITE). Now, most teachers will have some understanding of the term and, in institutions which undertake school-based ITE, many staff will have had some involvement, however fleeting and informal. When headteachers and mentors are asked to estimate the extent of teacher involvement in mentoring, the number always extends far beyond those with a designated role in ITE (Barker *et al.* 1996). Since schools often rotate the role, some teachers will have had transitory experience of mentoring while colleagues may be preparing to take on the role. Others will have had informal mentoring experience by virtue of the fact that student teachers have been placed in their departments or because a student has been attached to their form group. Yet others will have made an input to the wider professional development programme which the school provides. In schools engaged in school-based ITE, the scale of teacher involvement is considerable and extends far beyond those with official roles in the process. For this and for other reasons, the mentoring population is a shifting one, with teachers moving in and out of the role as their job and school circumstances change. In discussing the attempt to forge a partnership between schools and higher education institutions (HEIs), Alexander (1990: 59–60) pointed out that:

> . . . we have here a problem which by its nature can never be solved once and for all, because partnership, however institutionalized, ultimately depends on human relationships, and these have to be learned afresh and sustained by individuals.

The point applies no less to mentoring, in that relationships, roles and skills are in a constant process of regeneration and review via the flux of individuals. We hope to help to meet this ongoing need in this book.

There is a second purpose which this text is intended to serve. School-based ITE for secondary teachers was only fully implemented in September 1994, although there had been initiatives and pilot schemes in operation before that date. In any new policy initiative, there is a potential discrepancy between implementation at what Alexander (1990) has described as the *enabling* and the *action* levels. The enabling level is the formal level of structures, designated roles and procedures, and tends to involve those who have a managerial or liaison role in relation to the initiative (e.g headteachers and coordinators in the HEIs). The action level 'comprises the day-to-day interactions of the various individuals and groups who operate at the cutting edge of the teacher education process: students, tutors, and the teachers and pupils' (Alexander 1990: 60). For a variety of reasons, there is often a gap and sometimes a gulf between what is planned for, and intended, at the enabling level and what actually happens at the level of action. This text focuses on the translation of the policy for school-based ITE from the formal, documented level to the practical level of action in schools. Therefore, it sometimes exposes a discrepancy between the rhetoric of ITE and its implementation but always with the intention of heightening awareness of problems and possibilities, and of contributing to the informing and improvement of practice.

An important feature of the text is the use made of research findings, quotations from practising teachers reflecting on their experiences as mentors and case studies which capture some of the issues in mentoring in the form of particular, personal situations. Because of its concern with practice, problems and possibilities, this book is intended to contribute to the work of schools and teachers who are at various stages in their involvement with school-based ITE, including those who are considering involvement, those who are preparing to introduce school-based ITE and those who are already experienced but are seeking further professional development in this area. In taking this approach, we hope that the book can make a contribution to teachers' own professional development as well as to that of student teachers. We believe it is important for this to happen because, without it, there is a danger of uncritical and unreflective reproduction of practice and philosophies (cf. Menter 1989). Consequently, the book does not comprise a collection of 'tips for teachers'. Theoretical issues are covered, not least because teachers now have responsibility to make explicit to their students links between theory and practice.

At this point, it seems appropriate to emphasize that we recognize that every school is, in many respects, a unique community. Specific details vary, as do personalities. What works in one setting will fail in another. Readers should therefore constantly bear this in mind when considering applicability to their own institution.

Terms of reference

Both Val Brooks and Pat Sikes are professional tutors at Warwick University Institute of Education and this text grew out of the university's

'PGCE Mentor's Guide'. Its origins are reflected in certain sections which make reference to Warwick initiatives or use materials derived from the guide. However, the intention has been to produce a text that is meaningful for mentors working in partnership with other HEIs. Therefore, an attempt has been made to broaden the terms of reference by not tying the text too closely to a particular scheme. Where reference is made to Warwick, the material is used for the purpose of illustration only. This book is intended to supplement, rather than replace, any local guidelines and training. It is suggested that it is able to do this because there are generic mentoring skills and fundamentally similar training situations. However, this is not to deny the differences in the detail of individual schemes.

Perspectives on the mentoring experience are also broadened by including commentary not only from practising mentors but also from headteachers, student teachers, HEI tutors and teachers with only an informal involvement. This helps to elucidate the experience from different standpoints and to create a fuller sense of the total process of mentoring. Nevertheless, the mentor remains the principal focus of attention throughout. We have access to material from this varied range of sources because of our own involvement in mentoring research projects. For instance, Val Brooks has undertaken two separate studies since Circular 9/92 (DfE 1992) was published, one involving 150 mentors and a number of student teachers working with the Warwick school-based partnership, and the other a large-scale survey involving over 400 teachers (including headteachers, mentors and teachers with an informal involvement in mentoring) in 200 secondary schools throughout England and Wales (Barker *et al.* 1996). In total, these schools were working in partnership with at least 16 separate HEIs. Thus, the experiences of well over 600 practising teachers, most of them mentors, inform the text.

The book confines itself to secondary ITE, concentrating in particular on the postgraduate certificate in education route to qualified teacher status. It is also concerned with school-based rather than school-centred initial teacher training (SCITT) schemes. However, primary colleagues and those involved in SCITT programmes and undergraduate courses may find that the general principles as well as some of the detailed suggestions have pertinence to their own situations. Whether to refer to the preparation of beginning teachers as ITE or ITT (initial teacher training) is an ongoing issue. This text uses both terms. However, we prefer ITE because it suggests a preparation that is broader and more intellectually orientated than ITT, which suggests a narrower focus on task-related skills. We believe that teachers are best educated not trained. However, the term of preference in government documents is ITT. Where appropriate, this term is used.

The text focuses on schools as the sites for school-based ITE but not exclusively so. Since the current system (DfE 1992) is premised on a partnership between schools and higher education, there are times when reference to higher education is necessary to convey a sense of the different elements which comprise that partnership. However, reference to higher education is made only when its omission would distort or mislead. Issues regarding quality assurance and the monitoring of standards clearly loom large given the greater disparity of student teacher experience on mentoring schemes as compared with traditional forms of ITE (Reid *et al.* 1994) and the way in which all aspects of education are increasingly subject to the scrutiny of external agencies. These are brought to the fore as critical areas to be addressed.

The book says very little about the pupils in schools involved in ITE. Inevitably, any decisions that are taken – from the initial one to join a scheme through which classes are to be taught by students, to whether or not a student should pass – are dependent upon the significance for pupils' learning. The fact that pupils are not explicitly mentioned very often does not mean that they are not seen as crucial stakeholders in ITE.

The format of the book is as follows. Chapter 1 places mentoring in context by examining different models of partnership between schools and HEIs and exploring their implications for the teacher education process. In Chapter 2, models of mentoring become the focus of attention. Different models are presented and their relationship to different traditions of teaching and teacher education are discussed as well as associated mentoring strategies. Having provided a conceptual framework in Chapters 1 and 2, Chapter 3 moves on to the more functional requirements of school-based ITE: the definition of roles and responsibilities. In Chapter 4, mentoring is considered as a management issue. Approaches to the management of school-based ITE are presented. Students are the focal point in Chapter 5, which suggests ways of working with beginning teachers. Assessment is the subject of Chapter 6, which looks at some technical requirements of assessment as well as acknowledging some of the problems and possibilities associated with the assessment of teaching competence. Finally, Chapter 7 considers strategies for increasing the effectiveness of the mentor. We have cross-referenced the text so that those readers who wish to use the book selectively may do so.

As well as quotations, which are incorporated into the text, some chapters are supported by case study materials, which appear at the end of the associated chapter. The case studies could have various uses depending on the mentor's starting point and purposes. At one level, they stand as illustrations of some of the analysis presented in the text, but they could also be used in professional development activities providing a stimulus to discussion and debate. They could provide: material for use in the induction programme for new mentors; a starting point in formulating school policies on ITE; the basis for team development exercises and continuing professional development for existing or returning mentors.

At the time of writing, school-based ITE partnership schemes were working to the 9/92 competences (DfE 1992), but revised competence definitions may well be introduced by the Teacher Training Agency in the future. However, the general principle of competence-based ITE will remain the same regardless of precise detail.

1 THE CONTEXT OF MENTORING

Chris Husbands

Introduction

Student teachers have always learned to teach in classrooms (Cohen and Manion 1989; Gardner 1993). For many years they have gone into schools for classroom experience, to learn the tools of their trade through teaching practice. 'Surviving' on 'teaching practice' is one of the rites of passage for all student teachers. The prospect arouses feelings simultaneously of excitement, anticipation, insecurity and fear, for it brings student teachers face to face with the routine which will form the staple of their professional lives. In place of the ordered certainties of the lecture hall and the seminar, teaching practice is built on the daily unpredictabilities of the classroom. In place of idealistic planning there is the pressure to develop coping strategies to 'get through' a lesson, a day, a week, a half-term. The rhythms of teaching practice, furthermore, have traditionally been marked by the cadences of supervisory or assessment visits by a tutor: at worst, an ordeal, in which classroom teachers might be allies ('I'll take Graham and Siobhan out and work in the library when your tutor visits') or complicit in conspiratorial discussions about the student ('I must have a word with your tutor before she leaves'). School-based models of initial teacher education (ITE) subvert these rhythms of teaching practice. Instead of the forewarned visits of the tutor, there is the almost constant presence of the mentor. Instead of the periodic assessment which accompanies a tutor's visit, there is the ongoing, often informal, assessment carried out by teacher colleagues.

How did we get here? What is the logic of school-based teacher education? There are at least two different narratives to be outlined of the context which has produced the movement away from higher education-based models of ITE to school-based models. One of the narratives is straightforwardly political and ideological, the other is professional and educational. Although it makes sense to deal with them separately, they intertwine at various points and, as a result, have produced a variety of local models of teacher education which may develop, over the next few years, in markedly different ways.

The political development of school-based teacher education

In January 1992, the Secretary of State for Education, Kenneth Clarke, spoke to the North of England Education Conference. His theme was 'concern about whether new teachers are being adequately trained in the right way for success in the classroom' (Clarke 1992: para. 15; cf. HMI 1988). Clarke argued that 'the whole process of teacher training [*sic*] needs to be based on a more equal partnership between school teachers and tutors in institutions, with the schools playing a much bigger part'. The *ideological* impetus underpinning Clarke's speech derived particularly, though not exclusively, from the activities of New Right pressure groups since 1979, which intensified after 1988. Clarke went on to outline four specific policy changes, in the first place confined to the preparation of secondary school teachers and later extended to primary teachers. The first was that teacher education should be based on a 'partnership in which the school and its teachers are in the lead in the whole of the training process' (Clarke 1992: para. 22). Secondly, teacher education should be predominantly based in 'those schools in this country which command the greatest confidence in academic and other aspects of measured performance . . . such as academic results, staying on rates, truancy rates and the destinations of pupils' beyond school' (para. 32). Thirdly, Clarke proposed extending the amount of time spent in schools by student teachers from the then minimum of 90 days to four-fifths of the course (para. 33). Finally, a change was proposed in the assessment of new teachers, based on a competency framework which set out the 'specific knowledge, understanding and skills needed by the newly qualified teacher' (para. 36). In concluding, Clarke acknowledged that such an agenda for teacher education meant that, 'for many institutions and for schools significant changes will be involved', not least since 'as more of the responsibility for teacher training moves from the colleges to the schools more of the cost of that training will move with it' (para. 39).

This was a *political* initiative to reshape ITE, and it elicited a series of political responses. One teacher educator described it as 'the political rape of teacher education' (Gilroy 1992: 6); a second argued that there were 'values threatened by the proposal to locate 80% of teacher training in schools . . . At stake [are] the spaces which enable student teachers to systematically reflect about the difficult and complex task of educating children' (*Times Educational Supplement*, 7 February 1992, p. 18). In key respects, however, Clarke's initiative was an episode in the development of Conservative policy on teacher education rather than a new departure.

Throughout the 1980s, the Thatcher government had pursued changes in teacher education designed to make ITE more 'relevant' by shifting responsibility closer to the classroom. In Circular 3/84, the DES established the Council for the Accreditation of Teacher Education, for the first time giving a Secretary of State the right to influence the detailed structure of ITE, and proposing that: '[Higher Education] Institutions in co-operation with local education authorities and their advisers should establish links with a number and variety of schools, and courses . . . should be developed and run in close working partnership with schools. Experienced teachers . . . should be involved in the training of students within the institution' (DES 1984: para. 3). In 1989, the Secretary of State for Education paid tribute to already established school-based courses, welcoming 'the increased emphasis on work in schools – not just teaching practice but more formal study too, so that teachers in the schools are more involved in the whole training process' (Baker 1989: para. 37). The revisions to Circular 3/84 proposed in DES Circular 24/89 went further by not only suggesting that teachers should be involved 'in the planning of initial training courses and their evaluation', but also requiring institutions to have 'a written policy statement which sets out the roles of tutors, head teachers, other teachers, employers and students in relation to students' school experience' (DES 1989a: 5).

Paralleling such developments were the introduction in 1988 and 1989 of the 'licensed' (DES 1988) and 'articled' (DES 1989b) teacher schemes. The 'licensed teacher' scheme introduced 'on-the-job' training for entrants over the age of 26 and the 'articled teacher' scheme brought in two-year training programmes for graduates. Both schemes were school- or LEA-led, and were partly a pragmatic solution to problems of teacher supply and retention as well as steps in the progressive removal of ITE from the control of higher education. However, they were also based on the assumption of workplace-based rather than higher-education-based training: trainees would learn on the job where they would 'undertake such training as the employer deemed appropriate' (DES 1988: para. 14). In short, then, the policy initiative towards enhancing the responsibility of schoolteachers in teacher education, developed in 1992, was simply an extension of policy initiatives deployed throughout the 1980s; indeed, the figure of four-fifths of trainees' time spent in the classroom was derived from the articled teacher scheme.

Clarke's initiative was subsequently modified in important details before his successor as Secretary of State for Education, John Patten, implemented it. For example, the proportion of time student teachers were to spend in schools was reduced from 80 to 66 per cent. In other respects, the pace of change in ITE quickened. Higher education institutions (HEIs) began to work on the detail of developing and agreeing funding arrangements for school-based partnership models of ITE as required by Circular

9/92. By 1994, all HEI-administered secondary ITE was based on 'partner-ship' models in which students spent at least two-thirds of their time in schools and HEIs passed on up to a third of their total funding. Other commentators have pointed to a radicalization of the Conservative educational agenda after 1991 (Husbands 1995a; Ranson *et al.* 1995) and teacher education was not excluded. In Circular 14/93, a somewhat adapted model of school-based teacher education was extended to the preparation of primary teachers on both one-year postgraduate and four-year undergraduate courses (DfE 1993a).

On another front, the Open University was asked to develop a distance-learning teacher education programme under which students applied directly to schools who then worked with the students using distance learning materials (Moon and Shelton Mayes 1995a, 1995b). Under pro-posals introduced in 1993, which were subsequently incorporated in the 1994 Education Act, the Teacher Training Agency was established. This enabled funding for ITE to be separated from the rest of higher education (Furlong 1995). More significant was the Act's legal confirmation that con-sortia of schools could mount their own school-centred initial teacher training (SCITT) programmes without reference to higher education (DFE 1993b). By 1995, some 600 students a year were being trained by SCITT consortia.

Ideological pressure, particularly from the New Right, has underpinned these policy developments towards workplace-based training for new teachers. Such formulations would expel HEIs from the process of teacher education entirely, and meant that much of the debate about school-based training was confused by ideological concerns (Furlong 1992). There were changes in ITE in the 1980s but, even following these, New Right com-mentators continued to argue that ITE remained too theoretical. New Right authors were critical of the nature and practice of HEI-administered teacher education as they perceived it. Letwin went so far as to say that 'the fact is that the teacher training system to a great extent embodies the ideas and methods which have made British maintained education the laughing stock of Europe' (Hillgate Group 1989). In a similar vein, Lawlor (1990: 7) wrote that '[new] teachers are not encouraged to develop the style of teaching which time and experience prove best for them'.

This was not simply a result of the supposed failings of teacher edu-cators, although Lawlor (1990) and O'Hear (1988) in particular were highly critical of them. Some critics attributed the so-called problems to a structural failing of higher-education-based teacher education. Since teaching was *by definition* a 'practical activity', schools alone were able to train new teachers by exposing them to opportunities to observe experi-enced teachers and undertake practice (Lawlor 1990: 8). For such com-mentators, changes set out in Circular 9/92 simply did not go far enough. Lawlor (1990: 38), for example, had proposed that 'graduates . . . be sent to the schools to train on the job . . . [and] existing education departments should be disbanded' (for a detailed commentary, see Wilkin 1996: 161–5).

The professional history of school-based teacher education

The advocacy of school-based ITE has not been confined to the New Right. In the period following the Second World War, a grounding in 'theory' which could be 'put into practice' was seen as essential for teacher education. Yet 'theory', comments Wilkin (1990: 6), was widely perceived as 'a disaster area . . . The failure of theory to provide the answers to the problems of the classroom had forced a reconsideration of its value within the curriculum'. Quite separate from a response to the New Right critique, there had been a marked shift in the conceptualization of the place of theory in ITE in the late 1970s and early 1980s. In place of a theory-grounded initial training curriculum defined in terms of the 'disciplines of education', there emerged a 'radical' conception in which:

> Theory was no longer only a body of research-based knowledge to which reference could be made in times of trouble. It was, alternatively and additionally, articulated 'craft knowledge' [which] emphasises theory-as-process . . . 'it is the practitioner who is expert since he or she is the owner of a personal theory'.
>
> (Wilkin 1990: 7; see also Wilkin 1996)

This sort of approach informed McIntyre's analysis of the principles of the Oxford Internship Scheme in the mid-1980s. 'Internship' was an ambitious programme of teacher education established, with considerable financial support from Oxfordshire County Council, as a partnership between the University of Oxford, Oxfordshire LEA and Oxfordshire comprehensive schools (Benton 1990). Under internship, student teachers spent two-thirds of their postgraduate certificate in education (PGCE) year attached to a single school. Central to the scheme was McIntyre's (1988: 107) argument that, 'our long-term influence upon them (i.e. student teachers) can be greatest not so much by trying to persuade them of the merits of various practices but rather by helping them to make their judgements rationally and realistically'. The capacity for 'rational and realistic judgement' was to be developed 'by trying to ensure that each of them has a secure personal relationship with a mentor' (ibid., p. 111).

McIntyre (1988) explored the nature of the mentor–student relationship in interesting language: the mentor-based curriculum was not for him *fundamentally* about classroom competence *per se* or about the professional craft knowledge of the teacher, but rather concerned 'the explicit generation and testing of hypotheses, most typically hypotheses about what can be achieved by acting in given kinds of ways in given types of situation'

(p. 108). This description of hypothesis generation mirrors the sort of action-research which characterized approaches to in-service work with teachers (e.g. Elliot 1976), and which by the early 1980s were developing in ITE (e.g. Tickle 1987).

The second significant shift in curriculum development in ITE in the 1970s and 1980s was the increasing emphasis on 'partnership' between schools and higher education. As with 'theory', the root of the difficulty to which 'partnership' was a response, for McIntyre (1988: 105), was 'that student teachers frequently find . . . their courses irrelevant to the practical tasks which confront them in schools . . . that student teachers generally do not learn much, although there is a great deal to be learned, from their observation of the practice of experienced teachers'. The rhetoric of 'partnership' between training institutions and schools has been traced by Margaret Wilkin (1990, 1996) throughout the 1960s, 1970s and 1980s. She argued that 'it is clearly the case that it is in schools that the vast majority of [training in practical skills] must be done, and that primarily under the day to day supervision of school staff' (UCET 1979: 9–10; quoted in Wilkin 1990: 11). This had been going on, in some cases, for many years. For instance, in the 1960s, some teacher education institutions – notably the University of Sussex – had developed postgraduate teacher education programmes which were as much as two-thirds school-based. As early as 1972, the James Report had suggested that 'schools, and teachers in them . . . be asked to undertake new roles in teacher training . . . Teachers in schools . . . be more closely involved in planning and supervising practical work . . . be associated with the selection of students (DES 1972: para. 3.47). A decade later, Her Majesty's Inspectorate (HMI) proposed that 'partnership between schools and initial training institutions should be strengthened at all levels and in all aspects of the student's training' (HMI 1983: 17).

It is difficult to be clear about the extent to which 'partnership' models of training were adopted by teacher educators. In 1982, the School Partnerships in Teacher Education Project noted that PGCE 'tutors were clearly unwilling to give up their teaching practice responsibilities . . . [and] disagreed strongly that school staff should take the main responsibility for supervision' (Patrick et al. 1982: 197). At Oxford, in 1985, the developers of 'internship' could still think in terms of 'new roles for professionals in the University as much as in schools, new relationships between the two' (quoted in Pendry 1990: 42; emphasis added). Part of the difficulty was a lack of clarity about what 'partnership' or 'school-based' teacher education actually involved. The lack of clarity was revealed by the Cambridge research programme (Furlong et al. 1988). It is clear that in some versions, the term was simply deployed to describe ITE programmes which were substantially based in schools – that is, for more than 50 per cent of their time. In other versions, the term and the concept were deployed qualitatively to describe ways in which student experience in schools might be enhanced (Goodfellow 1992), since as Hirst (1991: 86) observed, 'without greater clarity on [the theory–practice relationship] the practice of training is likely to remain as "informal" a practice as much current teaching in schools'. A third characterization of the nature of 'school-based training' was one in which 'substantial tasks' in relation to training were delegated to teachers – most commonly the assessment of students' practical competence, and albeit less often shared responsibility for the design of programmes. Closely related to this, but given the exigencies of time far less common, was an understanding that school-based teacher education might allow for a careful definition of the 'different but complementary' roles of tutors and teachers in the task of training (McIntyre 1990).

Schools, higher education and 'practical professional education'

By the mid-1990s, the twin tracks of political change and professional dialogue have combined to alter, radically, the landscape of teacher education. Teacher education is largely school-based, distributed between higher-education-administered partnership programmes and a small but growing number of school-administered programmes. In practice, the different models of teacher education share many assumptions about the nature of student teacher learning. The purpose of teacher education in all forms of programme is principally to develop student teachers' competence as classroom practitioners by providing them with extensive access to pupils in classrooms. 'Theory' has been replaced in ITE programmes by a concern to develop what Furlong (1995: 7–9) has called 'practical professional training'. Key responsibility for the management of student teacher learning is borne by a school-based mentor, normally in the student's own teaching subject. While HEIs remain budget-holders for their programmes, substantial elements of funding are passed to schools to support the work of mentors.

Different approaches to the development of school-based ITE have generated quite different conceptions of what mentoring actually involves. In some models of school-based ITE – most obviously in SCITT consortia, but also in some higher-education-administered partnerships – mentors play *the* leading role in planning, managing and assessing student teachers' learning. In SCITT consortia, mentors are, *de facto*, teacher educators. Consortia may frequently buy in expertise and consultancy from higher education academics, but mentors carry out all the functions of classroom training: designing the curriculum; introducing students to planning, teaching and assessing; and providing feedback on practical performance. In some HEI-administered partnerships, too, academics do not visit students in school, the higher education institution having devolved to schools all responsibility for supporting students while on placement. At the other extreme are partnerships in which responsibility for considerable elements of student teachers' learning in schools rests with higher-education-based tutors, and particularly with subject tutors. Subject tutors continue to visit schools, to observe students teaching and to offer guidance on their progress. In these models, the skills of mentors chiefly consist in enhancing those informal aspects of support for students' work in schools which they traditionally undertook in earlier approaches to teacher education. Mentors introduce students to school policies, offer guidance on classroom strategies with particular groups or pupils, and provide day-to-day support. In many partnerships, their status and role are enhanced by virtue of their involvement in the assessment of student competence. Between these extremes lie a host of other arrangements, providing different definitions of the role, function and responsibilities of mentors. The degree of 'partnership', and the extent to which *effective* responsibility for teacher education has moved from higher education to schools, varies considerably. In part, this variation results from ways in which different interest groups have 'defended their territory' in the transition to school-based teacher education, but it also arises from different assumptions about the ways in which the effectiveness of different partners can be maximized as teacher education focuses more explicitly on classroom practice (Williams 1995).

The sheer force of this focus on practice, and the financial exigencies which have accompanied the transfer of substantial resources to schools in HEI-administered programmes, have raised in some quarters the prospect of whether higher education has any long-term role to play in ITE. Whether on the New Right (e.g. Lawlor 1990), in some quarters of teacher education (Beardon *et al.* 1992) or in some schools (Berrill 1994), it has been seriously suggested that the task of mentoring student teachers can be undertaken by schools without the support of HEIs. Although it is indeed the case that the focus of curriculum development in ITE over the last decade has shifted to the way in which student teachers learn in schools (Furlong and Maynard 1995; Williams 1995), this transition is more complex than simply about the 'transfer' of training functions to schools.

It is true that schools now provide a key environment in which student teachers will learn to teach. But the principal responsibility of schools remains the education of their pupils; teachers are primarily concerned to ensure that their pupils learn effectively, and they apply their pedagogic skills to attempt to bring such learning about. Because of this, schools are not *necessarily* particularly fertile environments in which student teachers can learn. As McIntyre (1994: 91) observed, 'the move towards more school-based ITE creates *only* an opportunity: few benefits will follow without other necessary steps'. Mentors have to take actions to ensure that student teachers are not only presented with learning opportunities but also that they are in a position to learn from these opportunities. The following points – developed from the work of McIntyre (1994), Stephens (1995) and Husbands (1995b) – outline some of the specific contributions which schools are in principle in a position to contribute to the learning of new teachers:

- providing opportunities to practice;
- providing access to effective and rapid feedback on professional development;
- coordinating student teacher programmes;
- contextualizing good practice;
- providing opportunities to 'collect' variations on teaching procedures;
- helping students to reflect on their own and others' teaching;
- setting realistic targets.

Few of these contributions flow *automatically* from the increased role of schools in ITE. They depend, first, on a commitment on the part of mentors in school to plan for and implement programmes of support for student teachers and, second, on a continuing institutional commitment to teacher education in schools. Given the principal concern of schools with the learning of pupils, rather than student teacher learning, there is ample empirical evidence to suggest that in the early stages of the transition from higher education to school-based ITE, schools depend on the support of HEI-based tutors (Hagger and McIntyre 1993; Evans 1994). Beyond this, there are other reasons to argue for a clear continuing role for higher education. As schools play an increasing role in ITE, the number of locations in which ITE takes place will multiply. There will be continuing need for monitoring and quality assurance, functions which can be efficiently and effectively carried out by institutions of higher education (Sikes 1994). There are other powerful reasons to suggest a continuing role for higher education in ITE in, for example, the following key areas:

- supporting schools and monitoring quality;
- economies of scale (e.g. in provision of educational resources);
- introducing students to the 'practical business of teaching' away from the complexities of the classroom;
- modelling good practice;
- broadening students' experience;
- programme management and accreditation;
- helping students sustain a 'critical discourse' about the values underpinning teaching.

In the longer term, there are also, as Furlong (1995a) argues, fundamental reasons of principle to suggest a continuing role for higher education in the preparation of teachers. The first is to do with teaching as a *profession* with links to research findings and an academic base. The second, and perhaps even more significant, is to do with providing opportunities for student teachers to *begin* a critical discourse about their development as teachers in diverse, often contrasting, settings in a powerfully value-laden profession. Not all teaching is effective and not all institutional practices are supportive of learning. The critical examination of practice is a central concern of higher education. If teacher education in the future does not preserve and enhance the opportunities for teachers at all stages of their careers to examine their own practices and the values of the institutions in which they work, then few of the potential benefits of school-based ITE will be realized.

2 EXPLORING SOME MODELS OF MENTORING

Introduction

Some readers will remember, and may indeed have acted as, 'teacher-tutors' to student teachers. This role was, in some senses, the precursor of the present-day teacher-mentor. Moreover, as Chapter 1 has shown, higher education institutions (HEIs) and schools have been developing closer training partnerships for much of the second half of this century. However, the fact remains that mentoring is a novel role in initial teacher education (ITE). As McIntyre (1994: 91) has stressed, 'Teachers who have supervised student teachers and who now become "mentors" have to see themselves as teacher educators and to realize that that is a very different task from anything they have previously done.'

Other occupations, such as nursing and various businesses, have made extensive use of mentoring, especially in the USA (Monaghan and Lunt 1992), but it came relatively late to English and Welsh ITE. Now, however, it is widely practised at different teacher career stages – in the induction of newly qualified teachers and newly appointed headteachers, for instance – but perhaps is most commonly used in the initial preparation of secondary school teachers. Increasing use of mentoring should not lead us to assume that there is also widespread agreement on what a mentor is and what a mentor does. Definitions of the term differ widely and its use in different contexts denotes quite different activities. As Allsop (1994: 46) observed:

> . . . ten years ago, who had even thought of using the term 'mentor' in a teacher education context? That is a short time in which to achieve coincidence in the conceptual understandings, institutional arrangements and forms of action which are contained within the term 'mentor'.

Despite the newness of mentoring and the variations in interpretation of the meaning of the term, it is nevertheless tempting to think of mentoring as *an* approach, *an* activity, which one undertakes when working with student teachers. This view of mentoring as a discrete, self-contained entity is encouraged by the way in which the literature has identified different models. Mentors are variously defined as the skilled craftsperson of the apprenticeship model, the trainer in competence-based models, or the reflective coach, critical friend and co-enquirer of the reflective practitioner tradition. Thus, readers might gain the impression that they should select the appropriate generic model from the range available and adopt it. There are also other, more particularized models. The better known among these include those developed by Anderson and Shannon (1988), the Oxford Internship Scheme (McIntyre 1990), Furlong and Maynard (1995) and Tomlinson (1995).

Rather than taking on any particular model, the line taken by this book is that mentors should select strategies from the various models according to students' needs and school contexts. This chapter aims to provide an overview of the different theoretical and empirically derived models to enable mentors to make informed choices.

Some models of mentoring in initial teacher education

The apprenticeship model and the mentor as skilled craftsperson

Historically, apprenticeship represents the first formal attempt to train teachers systematically. Used extensively during the nineteenth and early twentieth centuries, it was the means by which the pupil-teachers, destined to work in elementary schools, were trained. The pupil-teacher system embodied essential features of apprenticeship. Training was carried out on-the-job and involved trainee and trainer in a pupil–master craftsperson relationship. The novice was inducted into teaching by an experienced practitioner by 'sitting next to Nellie', observing the teacher at work and then attempting to emulate them. Trial-and-error learning featured prominently! Those who were 'successful' might eventually proceed to training colleges where they would pursue their academic studies and become certificated teachers. In the meantime, headteachers were expected to devote some time to furthering the pupil-teachers' personal education but practice, inevitably, varied and some pupil-teachers were treated as no more than extra classroom assistance. Implicit in this model was a dichotomy between the pupil-teacher's own academic study and the acquisition of teaching skill. There was little sense that the two may be intimately connected and, in reality, achieving either was a matter of chance. The individual's academic study was dependent on the conscientiousness of each headteacher and the acquisition of craft skill depended on the individual's ability to make personal sense of teaching from what they had observed and then attempted to imitate.

Apprenticeship is widely used in industrial settings for training in skilled trades. The key question is whether a mode of training useful in passing on lower-order craft skills is appropriate for education in the more intellectually demanding, higher-order professions? Attempting mechanically to reproduce what one had observed without developing insight into the processes at work proved to be an unreliable form of teacher preparation and the pupil-teacher system was abandoned. Teaching is not a collection of relatively simple craft skills which one can refine with practice and then apply in a hard and fast, formulaic manner in the classroom. There is not a single or a best way of teaching anything; rather, there is a range of possibilities and alternatives, some of which are better *per se* and some of which are more suited to particular circumstances. The capacities which a skilful teacher exercises are the product of a complex synthesis of personal values and beliefs, professional preparation and training, a store of relevant experiences and detailed situational knowledge. All of these may be deeply embedded in any of the actions which a teacher performs during the working day. Moreover, a teacher must be permanently ready to exercise professional judgement about what is appropriate in the flux of novel situations which constitute classroom life. If this analysis of teaching is accepted – and few educationalists would deny its validity – then the inadequacies of a pure apprenticeship system of preparation become obvious. First, unquestioning and slavish imitation of established practices does not give the learner access to the knowledge, understanding and judgement which underpin those actions and decisions – what Elliott (1990) has described as 'intelligent skill knowledge' (Furlong and Maynard 1995: 30). A reliance on learning from the observable, surface features of behaviour means that the learner may never penetrate their deeper meaning and significance. A second deficiency of this model is that it is conducive to professional stasis, for implicit within it is the notion of the experienced practitioner as infallible expert. Therefore, apprenticeship provides little or no opportunity for established practices to be challenged, refined or improved, nor for alternative practices to be developed and experimented with. Critics claim that it produces unthinking automatons who can reproduce behaviour but without intelligent skill knowledge or the possibility of further professional development.

Thus, history and experience seemed to have settled the question of the adequacy of the apprenticeship model of training teachers and, for much of the present century, educationalists have striven to evolve a system of teacher preparation which forges a meaningful relationship between on-the-job training and higher education. However, the question has been revived because there have been some, recently, whose simple view of teaching has made an apprenticeship system of training seem entirely appropriate. Right-wing thinkers such as O'Hear (1988) and the Hillgate Group (1989) have championed the apprenticeship model of initial teacher training (ITT). It has consequently become the model of mentoring that has been written about most frequently and most vehemently, largely because of the distaste which it inspires in educationalists and because those who *do* favour it have political influence. The feelings and attention which it has excited were intensified when the government launched the Licensed Teacher Scheme (DES 1988) (see Chapter 1). Fears were expressed that this scheme would herald the re-emergence of apprenticeship as a principal form of ITT. Apprenticeship was apprehended as a bogeyman which threatened to de-professionalize teaching.

With time, the challenge to professionalism, which apprenticeship and the Licensed Teacher Scheme represented, has taken on more measured proportions. Although there are few educationalists who would accept a pure apprenticeship model as the principal or the only form of ITE, the value of apprenticeship as one strategy among others is now widely recognized (e.g. Maynard and Furlong 1994; McLaughlin 1994; Tomlinson 1995). However, in place of the emotionally charged language of apprenticeship and its historical connotations, we have a more neutral term, 'modelling'. As described by McIntyre (1994), modelling is a cautious and a qualified version of full-blown apprenticeship. He asserts that 'focused and effective modelling':

> . . . can be used in deliberate and purposeful ways . . . teachers as teacher educators are very well placed to help student teachers focus attention on particular aspects of observed teaching from which they can usefully learn. In particular, they can help student teachers to recognize that they do not need to emulate teachers in their totality in order to learn specific and useful skills and strategies from them . . . teachers can make these aspects of their own teaching especially prominent and visible. Furthermore, they can draw attention to these aspects both in advance and in retrospect, so that student teachers can more easily observe them. It is not of course that one wants student teachers to imitate 'correct' ways of doing things: they each need to develop their own repertoires. What *is* needed however is the demonstration in concrete terms of what it means to achieve, for example, a busy working atmosphere, or clear understanding by pupils of what they have to do, and also the demonstration of some ways in which these things can be achieved. Student teachers frequently need to be offered the beginnings of a repertoire of ways of setting about basic classroom tasks.
>
> (McIntyre 1994: 87–8)

Thus modelling is now regarded as a strategy which is useful in certain circumstances and for certain purposes. It has a particular role to play at the start of a course where it may represent one step along the way to 'finding oneself' as a teacher and developing a professional persona

(Furlong and Maynard 1995: 183). Even at an advanced stage in a student teacher's professional development, modelling may still have a role to play. If there is a competence with which a student is experiencing difficulties or a skill which they are keen to develop to a higher level, then a teacher with recognized expertise in this area may model it for the student to study.

To sum up, few with a professional interest in ITE would countenance a pure apprenticeship model as an adequate form of preparation for beginning teachers. However, a more measured approach does not dismiss apprenticeship out of hand. It recognizes that when modelling is used *for* students and *by* students in a judicious manner for carefully thought-out purposes, it has a valuable contribution to make. This view is endorsed by Her Majesty's Inspectorate (DES 1991: para. 46).

The competence-based model and the mentor as trainer

In comparison with the apprenticeship model, less has been written about competence-based models in which the mentor acts as a trainer, although there are obvious connections and similarities between the two. For instance, on-the-job training features prominently in both, as does a relationship based on subordination. The trainer is seen as being in possession of skills and capacities into which the trainee must be inducted. The trainer in this model, however, bears a greater responsibility for providing a systematic programme of instruction geared towards producing pre-specified competences than was the norm with the traditional apprenticeship model of ITT. Moreover, under apprenticeship, the mentor is primarily a model who displays skill in relation to teaching rather than in relation to the mentoring role. In competence-based models, the training programme is likely to be fuller and more varied and the role of the trainer as an instructor who demonstrates and explicates pre-defined skills will be more fully and explicitly developed.

These models are, perhaps, best seen in the context of the movement to introduce competence-based education and training into higher education. Competence models are based on pre-specified behavioural outcomes and skill-related competences which the training and assessment procedures are tailored to meet. The job of the trainer is to devise a programme of activities which allows the trainee to fulfil the assessment criteria which may be detailed in a checklist of performance criteria and a profiling system. (A more detailed consideration of competence-based training and assessment is given in Chapter 6.) There are some who question whether such an approach is applicable to the professions and to higher education. Nevertheless, Circular 9/92 (DfE 1992: para. 2.1) specified a list of teaching competences which 'Higher education institutions, schools and students should focus on . . . throughout the whole period of initial training'. Although the way was left open for individual partnerships to incorporate the competences of Circular 9/92 into their own more elaborated programmes of training and assessment, there is no question of ignoring them or of adopting a totally different approach to education and assessment. The competence-based model is the official requirement and all ITE courses must demonstrate that they conform, to it to achieve accreditation. Thus, government policy offers a clear steer towards treating the mentor as a trainer. Indeed, government documents consistently refer to the preparation of beginning teachers as ITT not ITE (e.g. CATE 1992; DfE 1992; Ofsted 1993). This difference in terminology is a significant one in that 'education' implies something broader and more intellectually orientated than 'training', which suggests a narrower focus on task-related skills.

In summary, the competence model, in which the mentor performs the role of a trainer, is central to government thinking and provides the basis for the regulations with which all ITE courses must comply.

Mentoring in the reflective practitioner tradition

The final mentoring types which this chapter surveys are rooted in the reflective practitioner tradition. Ideas about reflective practice have been extremely influential both in characterizing the nature of teaching and in suggesting the kind of initial education which a teacher requires. A particularly influential figure in this field is Schön, who reached his conclusions about professionalism as a result of studying certain occupational groups, though not teachers. His studies of the working practices of these groups challenged the traditional notion of the professional person as an infallible expert who has been trained up to qualified status and, having achieved that level of expertise, simply practises the skills and exercises the specialist knowledge that were acquired during training. Schön found that two types of reflection played a much more central role in the thinking and practices of these occupational groups than could be explained by the infallible expert model of professionalism. He identified reflection-on-action (i.e. after the event) and reflection-in-action (i.e. during the event) as essential characteristics of this 'professional artistry', which was distinguished by its reference to a store of relevant previous experiences and detailed contextual knowledge rather than relying simply on the knowledge and skills acquired during initial training. It is not the purpose here to explore in detail the ideas of Schön and others who have been influential in making reflective practice so popular and widespread in our current thinking about teaching and teacher education. Rather, the aim is simply to sketch in enough background information to provide a meaningful context in which to place these more reflective approaches to mentoring.

On the basis of his studies of different professional groups, Elliott

(1991: 311–12) distinguishes between the infallible expert and the reflective practitioner models of professionalism as follows. Infallible experts:

1 Expect clients to defer to their superior knowledge and wisdom in
  identifying, clarifying and resolving their problems.
2 Engage in one-way communication. They tell and prescribe while the
  client listens and obeys. The client is allowed to ask questions from a
  position of deference but not to 'question' from a presumption of knowledge. There is little reciprocity in communication because the 'expert'
  is not concerned with developing a holistic view of the client's situation.
3 Understand and handle the situations they confront excusively in terms
  of the categories of specialist knowledge they have mastered.
4 Apply specialist knowledge intuitively rather than reflectively on the
  basis of the commonsense wisdom enshrined in the occupational
  culture.

Elliott (1991: 311) contrasts this model with 'the new professional images'
which are 'similar in many respects to Schön's (1983) characterization of
the "reflective practitioner" ' in that they involve:

1 Collaboration with clients (individuals, groups, communities) in identifying, clarifying and resolving their problems.
2 The importance of communication and empathy with clients as a means
  of understanding situations from their point of view.
3 A new emphasis on the holistic understanding of situations as the basis
  for professional practice, rather than on understanding them exclusively in terms of a particular set of specialist categories.
4 Self-reflection as a means of overcoming stereotypical judgements and
  responses.

Elliott (1991: 312–14) goes on to describe the reflective practitioner thus:

Rather than operating as an infallible source of relevant knowledge,
the role of the reflective practitioner is to participate in a process of
collaborative problem solving through which the relevance and use-
fulness of his/her specialist knowledge can be determined and new
knowledge acquired . . . From the perspective of the 'reflective practitioner' model professional competence consists of the ability to act
intelligently in situations which are sufficiently novel and unique to
require what constitutes an appropriate response to be learned *in situ*.
Competence cannot be defined simply in terms of an ability to apply
pre-ordained categories of specialist knowledge to produce correct
behavioural responses. Within this model of professionalism, stereotypical applications of knowledge are to be avoided and this implies
that any attempt to pre-specify correct behavioural responses or 'performance indicators' is a constraint on intelligent practice . . . Learning

to be a reflective practitioner is learning to reflect about one's experience of complex human situations holistically. It is always a form of experiential learning. The outcome of such learning is not knowledge stored in memory in prepositional form but 'holistic understandings' of particular situations which are stored in memory as case repertoires . . . In confronting a new situation, the practitioner selects cases from memory and compares and contrasts it with them. This eclectic use of past experience illuminates aspects of the situation which may be significant for clarifying the new situation and determining an appropriate response.

If one accepts these theories, learning to teach becomes a much more tentative, exploratory, context-specific, value-laden activity shaped in and through experience than pure apprenticeship or competence training models would allow. Other models of mentoring are necessary to accommodate this view of professionalism.

The mentor as a reflective coach

The coach helps the student teacher to use reflection as a tool for self-development. Following Schön's categorization of professional thinking into reflection-in-action and reflection-on-action, students are introduced to reflection-on-action as a principal means of learning on the job. Thus their own professional experiences become the basic material for learning about teaching. Tomlinson (1995) argues that students should be inducted into this kind of reflective practice from the outset by working alongside reflective practitioners who can model the skills for them. In this way, students become habituated to these ways of thinking and working, thus providing a sound basis for ongoing professional development once the course ends. The term 'reflective coaching' may be taken to imply a passive, contemplative role for the mentor. However, this would be misleading. Coaching is an active process which depends on the mentor making planned and systematic interventions into the students' reflections in order to make them more meaningful and analytical. Students will, of course, think about their teaching experiences with or without encouragement to do so, but without the support and guidance of more experienced teachers, too much of the learning that may be gleaned from classroom experiences is left to chance. A skilful mentor can extend novices' thinking about teaching by channelling them into fruitful areas for enquiry. The mentor can help them to sift the significant from the inconsequential and to focus on areas which merit further exploration, such as values and assumptions which need to be scrutinized. The mentor can probe ideas in order to deepen insights. Interpretations of events may be challenged so that learners are encouraged to examine alternative possibilities, thus broadening their perspective. One of the most important keys to learning in this way is the use of language in either written or spoken form. A number of studies have demonstrated the role which language plays in pupils' learning and this principle also applies to adult learners.

Words are one of the tools with which we think and the need to formulate our thoughts in order to vocalize them (or write them down) helps us to clarify partially developed ideas and understandings. So it is through the process of articulating their experiences that students can also deepen their insights into them. In other words, using language to reflect on experiences can actually enrich one's understanding of their significance. By talking through their experiences with a more experienced coach and committing their thoughts and ideas to paper, either as a preparation for discussion or following it, students are enabled to expand their understanding. This does not preclude the mentor from occasionally adopting a more didactic role in which knowledge and instruction are transmitted directly from expert to novice. New language and concepts may have to be introduced and the competences contained in Circular 9/92 (DfE 1992) must be fulfilled. Nevertheless, ultimately the students must take ownership of new knowledge, skills and concepts, and by relating them to their own experiences and expressing them in their own terms they will make the learning *meaningful* (Ausubel 1987).

This form of learning may involve the participants in working through a cyclical process akin to that involved in reflective teaching:

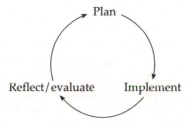

This cycle may be elaborated to incorporate various sub-stages, but the above three are the basic constituents of the reflective cycle, which is an ongoing, interrelated process, such that the reflection and evaluation which complete one cycle of experiential learning form the basis for planning in the next cycle. In the very early stages, a mentor can model this cycle and the associated skills for students to observe. Once a student has started to teach, the mentor's systematic interventions at the planning, reflection/evaluation and replanning stages are the basic constituents of reflective coaching which assist the student's reflection-on-action.

Gradually, students can also be encouraged to engage in reflection-in-action by a collaborating teacher or coach who works alongside the student in the classroom. This style of coaching is akin to the traditional sporting approach, by which sportspeople are helped to think about and refine their performances during execution by an actively involved coach who offers comments, instructions and tips.

This is probably the point at which we should concede that the different conceptions of mentoring presented in the literature are not as neatly pigeon-holed as the categories into which this chapter has been organized may suggest! In the literature, as well as in real life, the different models overlap 'untidily' and the same approach may be presented in one place as a fully developed model and in another as a strategy. Different authors also place approaches in different traditions. Coaching provides a particular example of this and several references may suffice to illustrate this 'conceptual overlap'. Modelling, for instance, clearly has its historical roots in the apprenticeship training of the pupil-teacher system, but it is also one of the strategies recommended by Tomlinson for use in reflective coaching. Tomlinson (1995: 38) explains the derivation of his model thus: 'which, following Schön, may be termed *reflective coaching'*. Thus, a form of mentoring (modelling) which is strongly associated with one tradition (apprenticeship) has also been embraced by the very different tradition of reflective practice. So strategies originating in one tradition may be 'borrowed' by another, quite different tradition even when those two traditions seem to be fundamentally opposed to one another. This reinforces the earlier suggestion that the notion that the models are discrete and mutually exclusive is questionable. Indeed, one of the particularized models described later in this chapter (Furlong and Maynard 1995) is, in fact, a composite of four generic models: model, coach, critical friend and co-enquirer. And Maynard and Furlong (1994) describe coaching as part of the competency model of systematic training. The purpose of this digression is to make clear that although the reflective coach is very much part of the reflective practitioner tradition, it incorporates strategies which, superficially, may appear to be at variance with the tradition and that this reflects the 'conceptual overlap' in the different versions of mentoring that have been developed.

Elliott and Calderhead (1994) have highlighted the importance of mentoring that strikes a careful balance between supporting student teachers and challenging them to promote professional growth. The final two reflective models which this chapter discusses are particularly appropriate to later stages in a student's professional development when basic competence has been established and the student is proficient in a limited repertoire of tried and trusted strategies. They aim to shift the emphasis away from – but not withdraw – support and put it instead on the need for challenge.

The mentor as critical friend

During the initial stages, beginning teachers tend to be self-centred, focusing inward on their own performance. To become more effective practitioners, they will soon need to make a fundamental shift in emphasis from centring on themselves as teachers to focusing on pupils as learners, and from seeing a lesson as a teaching opportunity for themselves to considering its learning potential for their pupils and allowing that to determine how they teach. When helping students to make this difficult transition from a performance-orientated student to a facilitator of learning, Furlong and Maynard (1995: 190) present the mentor as a 'critical friend' with a task that is 'doubly challenging':

> . . . they need to be encouraged to look critically at the teaching procedures they have established and evaluate their effectiveness. However, as they are often still extremely insecure about their teaching abilities, they also need considerable support if they are going to achieve this . . . The mentor needs to be able to challenge the student to re-examine their teaching, while at the same time providing encouragement and support . . . Two specific mentoring strategies are particularly pertinent at this stage of a student's development. First, students need to return to classroom observation but now focusing their attention very specifically on how pupils learn . . . A second strategy is to focus again on lesson planning. This might be achieved by asking the student to plan a lesson or sequence of lessons. The mentor can then focus discussion of the lesson plans on the content of the planned lesson rather than on the 'performance' of the student.

The mentor as co-enquirer

Whereas the apprenticeship and the competence training models are grounded in relationships of subordination, even the nomenclature of this approach – *co*-enquiry, *partnership* supervision and *partnership* teaching – suggests the more equal relationship between mentor and mentee. Whereas in the competence training model the training agenda is specified in advance, in co-enquiry priorities are negotiated with the learner playing a key role in identifying the focus for attention. Observation and collaborative teaching are key techniques in this model, as in others, but they are undertaken for distinctive purposes. A pioneering piece of work in this area was that of Rudduck and Sigsworth (1985), who described the implementation of the practice of partnership supervision.

In partnership supervision, the mentor observes the student's practice in the areas selected for consideration by the student and provides an evidence-based record of the practice for the two to consider. Again, the student should take the lead in analysing and evaluating the performance using the mentor's record of the event as the basis for discussion. As the term co-enquiry suggests, the mentor is not expected to tell the student what she or he, in the role of expert, thinks of the performance, to carry out diagnostic assessment nor to prescribe future action, for this should be a process of collaborative enquiry in which both might be expected to make discoveries. The mentor participates as an equal in the process of enquiry in the knowledge that she or he may also gain from an exercise which is close to action research. Partnership teaching is similar to partnership supervision in that the two work as more or less equal members of a team in the planning and development of resources, lesson delivery and evaluation. This strategy may, again, provide excellent opportunities for the professional development of both parties. For instance, their earlier discussions may have thrown up 'research questions' – untried approaches, untested hypotheses – which the two may experiment with in partnership teaching. Knowing that two teachers will be present in the lesson may provide the spur and the confidence to try things which either might be reluctant to attempt alone.

Given what has been said so far about co-enquiry, it is clear that this is a fairly advanced form of mentoring, which is brought into play once a student has attained core competences. However, even though in its pure form it would be inappropriate at the beginning of a course to give a learner such a directing role in managing their own progress towards qualified teacher status (QTS), nevertheless there is no reason why features of this approach might not be used sparingly and judiciously at an early stage in the course. For instance, in providing feedback on students' early attempts at teaching, an approach which focuses exclusively on telling students what is bad (or good) about their practice, and prescribing future actions without attending carefully to the students' understanding of the situation they have experienced, is unlikely to promote the best kind of meaningful learning (Ausubel 1987). Clearly, working with this model of mentoring, as with others, is more a matter of judging the *degree* of application which is appropriate in particular circumstances rather than selecting a mentoring type *per se*. Nevertheless, an emphasis on co-enquiry may pay particular dividends in the later stages of a course.

Studies of learning to teach have identified different developmental stages through which students pass, one of which is 'plateauing'. Once students have struggled through the survival stage and have discovered techniques which work for them and enable them to achieve the competence levels necessary for QTS, there is a natural temptation to 'play safe' and carry on practising tried and trusted approaches rather than taking the risks involved in striving for further professional development.

Co-enquiry is a way of encouraging students to move on and not to rest content with basic competence and a limited repertoire of practices. Placing the onus firmly on students helps them to accept ownership and responsibility for their own professional development and is likely to motivate them into the bargain.

Anderson and Shannon's model of mentoring

Anderson and Shannon's (1988) 'Towards a conceptualization of mentoring' opens by exploring the derivation of the term 'mentor', going back as far as its origins in ancient classical literature. An analysis of the character and role of Mentor in Homer's *The Odyssey* leads to a characterization of the mentor as a role model who is engaged in a process which combines intentionality, nurturing, insightfulness, support and protection. They go on to consider more recent definitions in different occupational fields. In these, the mentor is variously depicted as a more senior/experienced/ expert/older adult whose relationship with a more junior/inexperienced/inexpert/younger colleague is aimed at promoting the mentee's personal and professional development. These definitions place varying emphases on a range of mentoring activities: teaching, counselling, guiding, developing, advising, sponsoring, protecting, promoting, supporting, challenging, modelling and befriending. Anderson and Shannon (1988: 40) conclude that the definitions which they consider:

> . . . do not highlight as much as we think they should that (a) mentoring is fundamentally a nurturing process, (b) that the mentor must serve as a role model to the protégé, and (c) that the mentor must exhibit certain dispositions that help define the process.

Anderson and Shannon (1988: 40) go on to summarize their own conception of mentoring thus:

> First, we believe that mentoring can best be defined as:
>
> > a nurturing process in which a more skilled or more experienced person, serving as a role model, teaches, sponsors, encourages, counsels, and befriends a less skilled or less experienced person for the purpose of promoting the latter's professional and/or personal development. Mentoring functions are carried out within the context of an ongoing, caring relationship between the mentor and the protégé. (Anderson 1987)

The essential attributes of this definition are: (a) the process of nurturing, (b) the act of serving as a role model, (c) the five mentoring functions (teaching, sponsoring, encouraging, counselling, and befriending), (d) the focus on professional and/or personal development, and (e) the ongoing caring relationship.

Mentoring dispositions

Mentoring dispositions

Opening ourselves

Leading incrementally

Mentoring relationship

- Role Model: X is a model for Y.
- Nurture: X nurtures Y.
- Care Giver: X cares for Y.

Functions of mentoring

Teach:
- model
- inform
- confirm / disconfirm
- prescribe
- question

Sponsor:
- protect
- support
- promote

Encourage:
- affirm
- inspire
- challenge

Counsel:
- listen
- probe
- clarify
- advise

Befriend:
- accept
- relate

Mentoring activities

- Demonstration lessons
- Observations and feedback
- Support meetings

Expressing care and concern

Fig. 1 Anderson and Shannon's mentoring model.

The model is further elaborated in figurative form. Figure 1 specifies the mentoring dispositions which Anderson and Shannon regard as 'essential', ,as well as breaking down the mentoring functions into their constituent parts and identifying key mentoring activities.

Furlong and Maynard's model of mentoring

Whereas Anderson and Shannon's (1988) model of mentoring is theoretical and owes much to the etymology and history of the term 'mentor', Furlong and Maynard's (1995) model is empirically based. It grew not from a survey of the literature but from field studies of student teachers enrolled on ITE courses. It is grounded in the conviction that:

Like any form of teaching, mentoring . . . must be built on a clear understanding of the learning processes it is intended to support . . .

mentoring strategies cannot be developed in a vacuum . . . they must be built on an informed understanding of how students develop.

(Furlong and Maynard 1995: viii and 195)

Furlong and Maynard's is a staged model which depicts learning to teach as a series of overlapping phases in which mentoring strategies need to be carefully matched to students' developmental needs. We are warned that its presentation as a simple stage model should not be taken at face value, since the development of individual students is likely to be idiosyncratic. Therefore, the stages need to be interpreted 'flexibly and with sensitivity' (p. 181).

Furlong and Maynard's staged model

Beginning teaching
- *Focus of student learning*: rules, rituals and routines; establishing authority
- *Mentoring role*: model
- *Key mentoring strategies*: student observation and collaborative teaching focused on rules and routines.

Supervised teaching
- *Focus of student learning*: teaching competences
- *Mentoring role*: coach
- *Key mentoring strategies*: observation by the student; systematic observation and feedback on student's 'performance'.

From teaching to learning
- *Focus of student learning*: understanding pupil learning; developing effective teaching
- *Mentoring role*: critical friend
- *Key mentoring strategies*: student observation; re-examining of lesson planning.

Autonomous teaching
- *Focus of student learning*: investigating the grounds for practice
- *Mentoring role*: co-enquirer
- *Key mentoring strategies*: partnership teaching; partnership supervision.

Mentoring in practice: Model or amalgam of strategies? Some tentative conclusions

It is clear from the previous sections that the term 'mentoring' should not conjure up in our minds the notion of a single, multipurpose, catch-all activity. Since teaching is a complex, multidimensional skill, it follows that learning *how* to teach and the process which supports that are unlikely to be simple or single-faceted. Research into the ways in which student teachers develop and learn (e.g. Corbett and Wright 1994; Furlong and Maynard 1995) highlights the inadequacy of such a conception of mentoring. Good-quality mentoring is a complex, sophisticated and multi-faceted activity incorporating different strategies and requiring high-level skills.

The ways in which a teacher mentors students are likely to be influenced by a range of factors, including:

- training received (or lack of it);
- the model explicitly required or implicit in a particular partnership scheme;
- personal preference influenced by the mentor's own view of the role of a teacher;
- personal qualities and interpersonal skills;
- the nature of the personal relationship which the mentor has formed with the student;
- values and commitments;
- the different stages in the course;
- the capacities and needs of the individual mentee;
- the desired learning outcomes associated with a particular activity.

Some of these points deserve further elaboration.

Training received

Teachers sometimes receive limited or no preparation before taking on their role as mentors and a common complaint about the meetings which pass as training sessions is that too much of the time is devoted to the straightforward passing on of course details rather than to genuine professional development activities (Barker *et al.* 1996). One study which explored the ways in which mentors actually interpret this new role (Elliott and Calderhead 1994) reported that just as student teachers' attempts at teaching are powerfully influenced by preconceptions formed as a result of their experiences as pupils, so too teachers' attempts at mentoring are determined by their preconceptions of learning formed by their experiences as the teachers of children:

> . . . teachers need to change their traditional orientation to their role . . . Teachers' notions of learning are built on the fact that they teach young pupils. The mentors in this study indicated that they often thought of their mentoring tasks in terms of their teaching but realized the inadequacy of such a model . . . the relationships between a

mentor and a novice teacher do not presently find a parallel in schools. Training for mentors to recognize this fact is necessary.

(Elliott and Calderhead 1994: 186–7)

As has already been pointed out, mentoring is quite unlike anything which teachers have previously been required to do. Therefore, they do need professional development activities which help them to explore what is distinctive about their mentoring role. Without this, some will inevitably fall back onto previously formed but inappropriate conceptions of teaching relationships.

The model explicit or implicit in a particular partnership scheme

Course programmes sometimes have specific models of mentoring built into them and made explicit in their course documentation. For instance, the Oxford Internship Scheme is a two-phase process which requires different mentoring approaches at each stage: the diagnostic assessment which is central to phase one gives way to partnership supervision in the second phase (Hagger *et al.* 1993: 91). Reflective coaching and progressively collaborative teaching are at the heart of the Leeds University Secondary School Partnership Scheme, as described by Tomlinson (1995). At the other extreme, we have encountered course documentation which says little or nothing directly about the model of mentoring which is implicit in its pages. A recent survey of ITE courses found that a high proportion of those which made reference to an underpinning philosophy mentioned reflective practice, suggesting the popularity of this mode of professional preparation (Barrett *et al.* 1992). However, Calderhead (1989) has suggested that reflective practice features sometimes more as a fashionable slogan than as a well-thought-through philosophy of teacher education.

Personal preference and the mentor's views on the role of a teacher

Different models of mentoring are rooted in different views of teaching and of the experiences which one requires in order to develop that capacity. Thus, looking at models of mentoring without reference to conceptions of teaching is like planning a scheme of work without reference to the knowledge, skills and concepts which the scheme of work is designed to promote. If one believes that teaching is a collection of relatively simple craft skills which can be grasped by observing their 'surface' in practice and then applying them in a formulaic manner with the occasional tip to refine practice, then an apprenticeship model of training will suffice. If, on the other hand, teaching is regarded as a complex skill conducted in circumstances where each new situation is unique, demanding the constant exercise of judgement based on situational knowledge and a store of relevant experiences, then a pure apprenticeship model of training will not give learners access to the knowledge and understanding which inform a teacher's skill and judgement.

Personal qualities and interpersonal skills

The close personal relationships which characterize mentoring, and the fact that much of the work is conducted on a one-to-one basis, make it especially important for the mentor to possess appropriate personal qualities and good interpersonal skills. Plenty has been written reinforcing what common sense would suggest are the personal qualities which suit an individual to mentoring (e.g. honesty, openness, sensitivity, enthusiasm, sense of humour, organization, self-awareness and reflectiveness). Interpersonal skills such as the ability to listen effectively, to give criticism constructively and to empathize are equally important. Although there is a high level of agreement that mentoring *per se* requires good interpersonal skills, it is also clear that different mentoring strategies make differential demands. The master craftsperson demonstrating a skill to a watchful apprentice and then explicating that skill requires little in the way of advanced interpersonal skills to accomplish this task. The teacher acting as a critical friend or a co-enquirer faces a much greater challenge to their interpersonal abilities.

The personal relationship between the mentor and the mentee

Mentoring, as a form of training, has certain distinguishing features. One is its reliance on close, one-to-one relationships as a means of delivering education and training. It follows that the success or failure of the training may hinge on the quality of the personal relationship between the mentor and mentee. Many mentors find the close personal and professional relationships which they develop with students one of the most satisfying aspects of the experience:

> I would like to add how very much I have enjoyed being a mentor this year. Much of it has been rewarding and I was lucky enough to have two excellent students. We got on well together and have formed a real friendship.

> Job satisfaction . . . I personally gained great satisfaction from facilitating the development of student teachers. I also felt that having another adult to relate to and share ideas was very enriching.

> It is quite demanding in terms of emotional support that I felt I had to give them . . . The feedback from them at the end of the practice is

that they felt they got that support and they had in fact felt secure . . . but in order to make them feel that way I had to work quite hard . . . I thoroughly enjoyed it and I would recommend it to anyone . . . Watching them progress from the beginning of the practice through to the end for me was well worth it.

However, some relationships either never become established or, more commonly, break down at a later stage in the course. A careful match between the mentoring strategies employed and the needs of the individual student is one of the best means of establishing a sound *professional* relationship even if, *personally*, mentor and mentee have little in common.

The different stages in the course

Learning to teach is a developmental process with learners passing through different stages along the way. Authorities differ in the number of stages which they have identified in this process. For instance, the Oxford Internship Scheme presents it as a two-phase process, whereas d'Arbon (1994) identifies three distinct phases. Furlong and Maynard (1995) have detected four stages, although they acknowledge that these are more likely to be cumulative than discrete. Whatever the number of stages that students go through (and it seems reasonable to speculate that this may vary from individual to individual), the unalterable fact remains that students' needs will change with time. What a student requires during the opening weeks of a course will be quite different from what is needed in the closing stages. However, empirical research has shown that some mentors are inclined to adopt a rigid mentoring approach which they are reluctant to modify in response to students' growing independence. When this happens, relationships can founder and further professional development may be impeded:

Mentoring was identified as an aspect that could potentially hinder or assist growth. Many of the relationships experienced difficulty during the fourth term. It seemed that by this point the articled teachers had grown in confidence . . . they were really ready to take on more teaching in their own style. In some cases clashes arose as they began to attempt to establish themselves. The demands of the mentor's role had changed and the mentors needed to change with the articled teachers.

(Corbett and Wright 1994: 230)

Clearly, mentors need to be sensitive to the developmental stages which their protégées have reached and flexible in their own approach, incorporating more sophisticated techniques such as partnership supervision and co-enquiry as students progress. Diagnostic assessment and modelling may become less acceptable as the principal or the only forms of learning on offer as students grow in competence.

The desired learning outcomes associated with a particular activity

It is a basic educational principle that *how* we teach should be determined by the learning outcomes we wish our pupils to achieve. Such a funda-mental principle is no less applicable to student teachers' learning. At any given stage in a course, different strategies will suit different learning out-comes. Thus, it is unwise to suggest that, at a late stage in a course, a student will never engage in more 'preliminary' activities such as observ-ing a skilled practitioner modelling a particular skill. If, as part of partner-ship supervision, a student has identified a particular competence which they wish to develop to a higher level, modelling may be one of the strat-egies selected to attain that learning purpose. For this reason, it is better to think of mentoring strategies as cumulative rather than sequential and discrete.

Finally

If the above points are accepted, then the following become essential fea-tures of effective mentoring:

- The mentor is a new type of teacher educator not a clone of an HEI tutor operating in a different setting.
- Effective mentoring is based not on a single generic model but is a col-lection of strategies used flexibly and sensitively in response to chang-ing needs.
- Different stages in the mentoring process are likely to be cumulative rather than sequential. As the course progresses, the range of strategies employed is likely to expand and the balance between them is likely to shift.
- Mentoring is an individualized form of training, often conducted on a one-to-one basis, which needs to be tailored to the needs of the indi-vidual.
- Mentoring is a dynamic process, aimed at propelling students forward, which needs to combine support with challenge.

The way in which we have organized Chapters 2 and 3, with Chapter 2 exploring some models of mentoring and Chapter 3 focusing on roles and responsibilities, is quite deliberate, for as Anderson and Shannon (1988: 41) point out:

> In developing teacher mentor programs it is all too easy to focus pre-maturely on such tasks as designing job descriptions for mentors,

selecting mentors and protégés, providing some initial orientation sessions, and then getting a program underway. To do so, without first thinking carefully about the concept of mentoring, is to run the risk of developing programs that are incomplete, lack integrity, and duplicate programs that in some form have already been tried. We believe that those who develop mentoring programs for beginning teachers should embed them in a definition of mentoring that captures the essence of the mentoring relationship . . . Only when a strong and clear conceptual foundation of mentoring is established can effective mentor programs for beginning teachers be constructed.

Having explored these fundamental conceptual issues in Chapter 2, it is to the more functional issues of roles and responsibilities that we turn in Chapter 3.

Case study: Different approaches to mentoring – a student's perspective

Both of my parents are teachers and so my home was always full of talk about schools and education. People expected this to put me off of teaching but it didn't! I have a real passion for my subject which I want to share with others. I started the course with pretty firm ideas about what good teaching is like and the kind of teacher I wanted to be.

My first 'subject mentor' was the head of the department, a very experienced teacher in her late forties I would guess. Most members of the department had been there for a long time but there were two younger ones who were quite new to teaching. Almost as soon as I arrived, my mentor presented me with a programme for the serial practice. It was all mapped out for me. At the time, I remember feeling slightly uneasy about this. Looking back, I think I felt there was no room for me and my ideas in all of this. My tutor at the university had encouraged us not to be passive during the course. He said we should try to build on our strengths and interests. 'You're not in a position to demand but you can negotiate', he kept on saying! A lot of the serial practice programme consisted of observation. I soon got fed up with this. I didn't feel I was getting much out of it and I was itching to do some teaching. I had so many ideas which I wanted to try out! However, my mentor had a firm belief in the value of observation. On one occasion she even warned me against trying to run before I could walk. Most of the time I was expected to observe her or people in the department who had similar ways of working. I never did get to see the two new members teaching but, from talking to them, I could tell that they had some different ideas on teaching from her!

I was given my teaching timetable well before the block practice started and, again, everything was signed and sealed before I got to see it. Some of my friends in other schools were envious. They had to wait much longer for their timetables to be settled. I was given the schemes of work too. Everything was laid out in detail for me – what to do and when to do it. My mentor was extremely protective towards all of the classes I taught. She or another member of staff sat in on part or all of the lessons for most of the block practice. She seemed to want me to be a 'stand-in' for her who would do things exactly the way she did them and in the same sequence. At first, I tried suggesting some of my ideas and questioned certain things but, whenever I did, a tight, anxious expression would come on to her face and I came to see my ideas as an impertinence. Occasion-ally, she said doubtfully, 'Well, I suppose you could try it', but more often her response was more negative. There was so much to cover that term and my way of doing something would be very time-con-suming or it wouldn't work with that group or in that classroom. I started to wonder if my ideas were worth anything, although my tutor had been excited by some of them. Finally, I came to the con-clusion that the course was something that I had to get through and, since the school would be assessing me, I would try to do what was expected of me.

When I met up with the rest of the group at the end of the prac-tice, I told myself that I should be grateful, for my experience had been very different from that of some members of the group. My mentor had taken her responsibilities very seriously. She had put time aside every week to sit down and talk to me about how things were going. She had checked most of my plans and given me detailed 'crits' on what I was doing wrong in lessons and how to put things right. She was always very concerned for me and for the classes and everything was meticulously organized.

Things were different in my second school. During the first week, my mentor surprised me by sitting me down and asking me where I thought I was in terms of the course and the CATE [Council for the Accreditation of Teacher Education] competences and what I thought I needed next. I was taken aback by this and found it tough to try to analyse my own development in that way. It took a long time but, in the end, we planned a serial practice jointly. He also suggested team teaching several lessons at the beginning. Planning together was time-consuming and difficult to fit in but it was well worth it. Somehow it 'unpacked' a lot of issues around lesson planning in a way that had not happened for me before. There were some comical moments in the lessons when neither of us was sure who should do what next, but generally it worked well. Being able to observe for part of the time while still being involved in the lesson was really useful. I also appreciated the fact that my suggestions were always taken seriously. I realize now that sometimes he let me try things knowing that they were unlikely to be successful. But mistakes were always treated as learning opportunities and I also believe that he would never have allowed me to do something which was likely to end in disaster because he could be surprisingly firm at times. The highest point in the practice for me was definitely on the day when I left. He told me how much he had valued my contribution and that he had learnt some things from having me there. I felt that I had 'arrived' as a teacher and that I must have something to offer the profession if a more experienced teacher could learn from me!

Overall, I feel that if I had had a second mentor who was much the same as the first, I would have been much more of a beginner than I actually am. The first school protected me from myself. I was rarely allowed to experiment and learn from the results – good or bad. Some of the things that I had wanted to do in that first school might have been total failures and others could have worked. I wasn't able to find out the difference.

3 ROLES AND RESPONSIBILITIES

Introduction

Traditionally, schools have been the places where teaching practice – not teacher education – has taken place. Consequently, the role of practising teachers in initial teacher education (ITE) has been a nebulous one. Indeed, Her Majesty's Inspectorate (HMI) has characterized the traditional role of the teacher as 'the informal "guide and friend" ' (DES 1991: para. 50). Practising teachers were essentially adjuncts who lacked a clear sense of purpose in the professional preparation of student teachers. This is not to underestimate the attempts to forge more meaningful relationships between higher education and on-the-job preparation for beginning teachers which have occupied much of the second half of this century. As Chapter 1 has shown, by 1984 Circular 3/84 (DES 1984) had called for close collaboration between higher education institutions (HEIs) and schools in the conduct of ITE. However, as we have also noted, partnership operated on different levels: enablement and action (Alexander 1990). Empirical studies such as that by Booth et al. (1990) have exposed the discrepancy that could exist between partnership at the enabling level and partnership at the action level. In reality, the role of practising teachers in ITE has been underdeveloped and ill-defined. Of course, these are generalizations and, as such, they do not capture the variations in practice which existed up and down the country. Nevertheless, only a year before Circular 9/92 (DfE 1992) was issued, an HMI survey of school-based ITE (DES 1991) found that most schools were playing a variable but limited role, with higher education acting as the main provider. Genuinely school-based courses were few and far between.

Circular 9/92 (DfE 1992) changed all of that by insisting that, by 1994, schools must become the 'full partners' (p. 1) of HEIs, exercising 'a joint responsibility for the planning and management of courses and the selection, training and assessment of students' (p. 4). Students were also to spend more of their time on the premises of partner schools – two-thirds in the case of the one-year postgraduate certificate in education (PGCE; see Appendix for full details). For many teachers, the effect of these requirements has been to precipitate partnership from the enabling level to the action level of their day-to-day roles and responsibilities. Both the scope and the scale of teachers' new roles and responsibilities are little short of revolutionary.

Why is this chapter necessary?

It is a truism that people work to greatest effect when a task is informed by a clear sense of purpose. Systems, too, work better when the purposes of their different parts are well-defined and articulate with one another (e.g. Riddell and Brown 1991). These points have a particular pertinence to school-based ITE because, as is constantly emphasized throughout this book, the integrity of the training depends on a number of people from two separate institutions – a school and a HEI – working in harmony with one another. Even within a partner institution, the trainers often work in different parts of the establishment. If a system with this level of organizational complexity built into it – not to mention the potential for dislocation – is to operate effectively, it is essential that the protagonists should have a very clear and shared understanding of their own roles and responsibilities and how these fit into the overall scheme.

A major source of mentors' dissatisfaction with the arrangements of Circular 9/92 in their initial stages occurred where there was uncertainty about roles and confusion over responsibilities.

If I was to repeat the exercise in the near future, I believe I would need to be better informed about how the university operates.

More *information* as to what students will have covered at university to know what to expect and what to deliver ourselves. My work *must* dovetail with that of university tutors.

There must be more precision in requirements of role.

It was, perhaps, inevitable that in the initial stages some partnerships were poorly developed and partially communicated, not least due to the haste with which the new system was ushered in. An HMI survey (DES 1991) which had advised against the wholesale adoption of school-based ITE was followed a year later by Circular 9/92 (DfE 1992), which stipulated that the new requirements should be in place across the board by September 1994! The emphasis on speedy implementation exacerbated the inevitable teething problems in establishing new partnership arrangements.

Both within an institution and between partners, lack of clarity over who does what and when in relation to course management, delivery and assessment has the potential to frustrate the mentoring process, making it less effective than it should be. It may lead to overlap and a wasteful duplication of effort (something which we can ill-afford in busy schools) or to unintended gaps and omissions in the students' experience and the general unease produced by working in an atmosphere of uncertainty. One mentor confided that: 'When I first started doing it, I have a sneaking suspicion that some of the reasons I didn't find it quite so onerous is because I wasn't entirely aware of what was involved.' In contrast, when partners are fully informed about each other's contributions, they are able to work efficiently, planning their inputs to complement and coordinate with one another, confident in the knowledge that compulsory requirements and other important elements of the training are in place. In these respects, maturing partnerships appear to be improving:

> I think that over the last two years the communications with the universities have been much better and I also think that, within schools, there has been growing recognition that initial teacher training is extremely important and that our role within it is changing . . . As far as the communication of the universities was concerned, I think that has been getting better, actually, over the years. We have had more understanding of what it is we are all trying to do . . . and that has got a lot better again this year because in fact, certainly with the institutions we are involved with, we receive all the information and *all* mentors have received it . . . I think that's very important because, sometimes as a mentor, your students have come rushing in to you and said, 'Who do I speak to about equal opportunities?' and you are thinking, 'Oh, goodness, yes! I know who they should talk to but I wonder if we are going to fit it in?' Had we known it was coming, because this was when it was going to be tackled in the Professional Development Programme, then we would have been able to field that quickly . . . I think my feeling as a mentor was that it would have been more supportive for me had I had more communication with the ITT coordinator and, in the earlier stages, with the universities, but I do think that is beginning to change.
>
> (Subject mentor)

The Oxford Internship Scheme is one of the better known forerunners in the field of school-based ITE. In *The Oxford Internship Scheme* (Benton 1990) it is conceded that the definition of roles and responsibilities is 'necessarily fairly detailed' but it is recommended that:

> . . . anyone wishing to set up a similar scheme would be well advised to negotiate a similarly detailed package if it is to be successful. The

minutiae are important if roles are to be properly understood, perceptions shared and the possibilities for confusion minimised.

(Benton 1990: 170)

The premise on which this chapter is based, therefore, is that a detailed and comprehensive description of roles and responsibilities, which has been understood and agreed by the different parties, is fundamental to success. Furthermore, individual partnerships need to be able to demonstrate, for external inspection purposes, that quality assurance procedures have been built into their courses. The precise definition of roles and responsibilities is one essential feature of this quality assurance (Ofsted 1993: 5, 22, 31, 37, 40), but to convince inspectors that a *genuine* partnership has been forged, the parties need to be able to demonstrate much more than a shadowy idea of what their role partners are doing, why they do it and how their own work fits into the programme. In other words, they need to be able to show that partnership exists at the action as well as at the enabling level.

Beyond the minimum requirements laid down in Circulars 9/92 and 35/92 (see Appendix), organizational and practical details have been left to the discretion of individual HEI/school partnerships. This sensitivity to local conditions has produced a system in which no two schemes are exactly the same. Courses are differently structured with roles and responsibilities which are variously defined and distributed between school and HEI personnel. Wilkin (1990) has drawn a broad distinction between two types of partnership relationship: one based on 'equivalence', where both parties share responsibilities equally, and the other founded in 'complementarity' where responsibilities are distributed according to expertise but balanced overall. More recently, Bines and Welton (1995: 21) have detected moves towards greater integration. Even the nomenclature of school-based ITE underlines the variety, with teachers working under a bewildering range of titles on different schemes. This further reinforces the need for a particular scheme to be exact in its expectations of different role partners.

The fact that roles and responsibilities have been left open to interpretation may create the impression that this chapter is either redundant or impossible to write! In reality, it makes the need for a detailed and thorough consideration of the possible permutations all the more pressing. The aims of the following sections, therefore, are to describe both those generic features which characterize school-based ITE and to present for consideration those details on which individual schools and HEIs have to make decisions. The role descriptions which are provided are based on the Warwick Institute of Education (WIE) PGCE (Secondary) course. They are offered not as a blueprint to be adopted wholesale but as an illustrative operational model. As such, they provide a useful

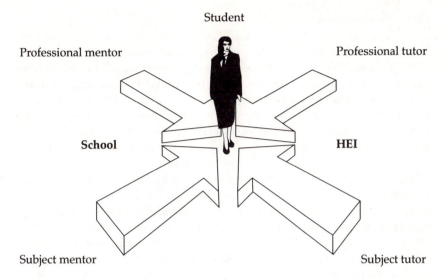

Fig. 2 School-based training roles.

starting point for the discussion of these issues. The final section, incorporating a case study and quotations, draws on the first-hand experiences of mentors to highlight issues which have been found to be critical in making these decisions.

Generic roles and responsibilities

Since partnerships differ in their detailed arrangements, it is not possible to provide exact descriptions of roles and responsibilities which apply across the board. Nevertheless, there are certain features which are sufficiently widespread that they may be regarded as characteristic of school-based ITE, even though they do not apply in every instance.

Many school-based partnerships treat ITE as the responsibility of four key individuals, whose roles can be presented in diagrammatic form (see Fig. 2). The terminology employed may be unfamiliar but, as has already been pointed out, there are no generally accepted titles for these roles. For ease of reference, the labels in Fig. 2 will be used throughout the text. (It is also possible to adopt an integrated approach to the delivery of subject specialist studies and further professional development. Where this approach is taken, it is usual for wider professional issues to be dealt with *through* students' subject specialisms.)

The professional mentor

Professional mentors are also known as senior coordinators, training managers, professional directors, coordinating professional tutors, central mentors, senior tutors, professional tutors, initial teacher training (ITT) coordinators, school coordinators and senior mentors. This list of titles is not comprehensive but is sufficient to provide a telling illustration of the differences in the detail of individual schemes. Nevertheless, several terms which are used by more than one partnership – 'senior', 'professional' and 'coordinator' – highlight certain generic features of the role.

The role is essentially one of coordination, with the professional mentor on most schemes accepting overall responsibility for the in-school provision for the group of students attached to the school. The professional mentor usually adopts an overview of the training and assumes an overarching responsibility for the consistency and coherence of the programme as it is experienced by students located in different subject departments. The professional mentor manages the evaluation and developmental aspects of the school-based programme. Liaison is an important feature of the role, with the professional mentor acting as the main link between the HEI and the team of subject mentors which he or she leads. For instance, the professional mentor inducts students into the school, follows their progress throughout their attachment and liaises over the school/HEI response should difficulties arise. He or she also coordinates the formative and summative elements of the assessment of students' teaching competence. As well as overseeing the management and administration of the school-based component of the course, the professional mentor usually has a specific responsibility for those parts of the course which deal with whole-school issues and students' wider professional development. Topics which are not subject-specific or which are cross-curricular generally fall within the remit of the professional mentor, although their subject application may be dealt with by the subject mentor. For instance, a professional mentor may lead a group seminar on the school's behaviour management policy. This may be complemented by individual sessions for subject specialists led by subject mentors which deal with the specific behavioural concerns of their subjects (e.g. safety considerations in physical education or in the conduct of scientific experiments). In some schemes, the professional mentor is involved in the setting and assessment of academic assignments.

Since the professional mentor role requires the ability to deal with whole-school matters and to take a wider perspective on educational issues, it is usually considered to be best undertaken by a senior member of staff with wide experience. It is a role frequently undertaken by deputy headteachers and vice principals and even by headteachers on occasion. It is uncommon for teachers occupying more junior positions in the school management hierarchy to assume this role.

The subject mentor

Alternative titles for this role include school mentor, geography / science (etc.) mentor, teacher tutor, mentor, subject tutor, departmental mentor, teacher mentor, co-tutor, designated teacher tutor and student mentor.

The subject mentor, who is located within the students' specialist subject department, accepts responsibility for a small number of trainees, rarely more than one or two at a time, since few departments are large enough to accommodate greater numbers. The department becomes the students' home base for the duration of their attachment to the school and its members should form a team which shares the responsibility for mentoring the students, albeit with the designated mentor in overall control. Thus, whereas the professional mentor has a coordinating and monitoring role within the school, the subject mentor performs these functions at a departmental level. The subject mentor inducts the students into the department and into subject teaching. He or she has responsibility for developing students' specialist subject knowledge, skills and application. Since there is a strong emphasis on developing students' classroom competence, the subject mentor arranges a programme of observation, discussion and practice teaching designed to introduce students to the range of teaching styles and practices within the department. It is usually the subject mentor who has the closest and most regular contact with students and deals with their development and needs on a day-by-day basis. The subject mentor contributes to the formative and summative aspects of the assessment of students' teaching competence.

This role requires an overview of the work of the department, its policies and its procedures and so it is usually undertaken by an experienced teacher who is involved in the department's management. Although teachers at all levels in the school management hierarchy become subject mentors, it is generally attached to a middle management role. Heads of department most frequently act as subject mentors, although those with responsibility allowances (e.g. second in department) also occupy the role.

The professional tutor

Based in the HEI, the professional tutor is the counterpart of the professional mentor and consequently also deals with whole-school and wider professional concerns. However, these role partners approach issues from a different perspective and, therefore, each has a distinctive contribution to make. The professional tutor complements the professional mentor's first-hand experience of a particular school by offering a broader perspective based on knowledge of a wide range of practices in institutions locally and further afield. The professional tutor should be familiar with the findings of research and development work and is likely to be actively engaged in both. He or she is able to draw out the principles and theoretical perspectives which underpin practice and thereby to enrich it. The professional tutor helps students to reflect on and share their learning experiences away from the hurly-burly of individual schools and, by adding his or her own expertise, extends their understanding. Whereas students will be attached to more than one school during their training (a requirement of Circulars 9/92 and 35/92), the professional tutor usually maintains contact with the group of students and/or schools throughout and is able to monitor progress. The professional tutor may also perform certain administrative and pastoral functions for the group. The relative distance and objectivity of the professional tutor contrasted with school-based personnel allows him or her to play a mediating role should difficulties arise with a particular student placement. Likewise, the tutor's breadth of experience of schools and students gives him or her a distinctive role in the assessment process, particularly in the moderation of standards across schools and in the final decision about students who are at or near the pass/fail borderline.

The subject tutor

The subject tutor has many attributes in common with the professional tutor. The subject tutor, based in the HEI, is the counterpart of the subject mentor and is concerned with the development of students' subject knowledge, skills and application. The subject tutor provides students with the principles and theoretical framework which the school-based work can extend, complement and particularize, giving concrete expression and practical experience of areas covered in theory. Involvement with research, curriculum development work and relevant subject associations should afford the subject tutor a wide knowledge of alternative practices. The subject tutor helps students to extend their subject expertise away from busy classrooms. He or she gives continuity to the subject component of the course by maintaining a link with a group of students and/or schools throughout the training. The subject tutor may also be called upon to perform a mediating role where difficulties arise between a student and a subject department and to contribute a wider perspective to the formative and summative assessment of a student's teaching competence.

The student teacher

At the centre of Fig. 2 stands the student teacher and yet, as Mountford (1993: 34–5) has pointed out:

> ... the role of a key partner, the ITT student, is often neglected. If ITT students are to act responsibly and autonomously then the ITT experiences need to prepare the student for this role. Involving the ITT

student more actively in their own development is critical in this regard . . . HEIs and schools . . . need to acknowledge the role that students [only] can play in their professional development and learning. [This] extends the partnership into what HEIs and schools can do *for* (rather than to) the developing teacher.

Student teachers should be recognized as key partners in their own preparation and encouraged – indeed, expected – to take responsibility for aspects of their own learning and assessment. All too often, students are passive, seeing the course as something which is done to them by others. From the outset, the expectation that they accept joint ownership of their professional development needs to be communicated. They should be helped to be proactive in seeking the experiences they need to further their own development and the school's ITE programme should be sufficiently flexible to accommodate an element of student-initiated learning. Chapters 5 and 6 look in more detail at these important issues.

The specification of roles and responsibilities

The following specifications are based on WIE's secondary school partnership arrangements. They illustrate how one HEI/school partnership has operationalized the professional and subject mentor roles and responsibilities.

The professional mentor

It can be reasonably expected that professional mentors will:

- be members of school staff with wide experience;
- be open to ideas and willing to examine critically their own practice and that of others through a process of analysis and reflection;
- be abreast of developments in their own areas of expertise and of education in general;
- be well versed in whole-school policies;
- exhibit a positive attitude towards the students and be supportive, while expecting the highest possible standards.

The professional mentor will also:

- coordinate the school experience of the whole group of students;
- lead the team of subject mentors appointed for the placement;
- work with the professional tutor to carry out a programme based on professional issues and whole-school themes.

The professional mentor is supported by the professional tutor, who focuses upon wider practice, principles and underlying theory. The professional mentor agrees an induction programme with the university tutors and students and also monitors students' progress in consultation with subject mentors and university tutors. The record of professional achievement (ROPA) is central to the negotiations between all partners about the progress of students.

The professional mentor has responsibility for:

1 The induction of students
   • Providing students with information about the school, its ethos, the local community and pupil intake (e.g. the school prospectus, staff handbook, timetable, calendar of events, policy documents, etc.).
   • Informing students about domestic arrangements and routines (e.g. staffroom procedures, lunchtimes, breaktimes).
   • Introducing students to the management structure and to key members of staff (e.g. headteacher, deputy heads, heads of year, heads of department, subject mentors and non-teaching support staff).
   • Guiding students around the school.
   • Drawing the attention of students to the pastoral system and school rules, including the use of rewards and sanctions.
   • Outlining expectations about the professional involvement of students as appropriate (e.g. staff meetings, parents' meetings, assessment procedures, report writing, tutor groups, etc.).
   • Informing students about school reprographic facilities, the availability of audio-visual equipment and information technology resources and booking arrangements for them.

2 Participation in the school/university programme
   • Planning a structured serial practice with the professional tutor and subject mentor; for example, observation in a variety of departments, tracking a pupil; shadowing staff in different roles; teaching individuals, small groups and classes for part or all of a lesson alone or as part of a team; placement with tutor group and year or pastoral team.
   • Liaising over course content and timing with the professional tutor and subject mentors.
   • Becoming fully aware of the nature of the practice and its place in the course.
   • Designing school-based elements of the course and, where appropriate, leading these (e.g. running seminars and activities on whole-school and wider professional development themes).

- Working with the professional tutor to evaluate the course and participating in professional development activities.

3 Acting as a team leader
- Leading the whole-school team of mentors (e.g. arranging meetings for the purposes of planning, developing, sharing, problem-solving, monitoring and trouble-shooting).
- Disseminating information about the partnership within the school and the local community (e.g. to students, colleagues, non-teaching support staff, pupils, governors and parents).
- Observing the practice of students according to course guidelines and when requested to do so by other mentors or tutors.
- Arbitrating where problems arise between subject mentors and students, involving subject or professional tutors as appropriate.
- Coordinating formative and summative assessment and the process of recording achievement.
- Maintaining an overview of each student's progress and reporting to the headteacher and university tutors where serious concerns arise about a student.
- Organizing extra support for students in difficulty.
- Reviewing and evaluating school procedures related to the students' experience (involving the professional and subject tutors, subject mentors and students).

4 Contributing to assessment and to the completion of the record of professional achievement
- Meeting with each student to discuss their achievements in school and to negotiate an action plan which addresses strengths and weaknesses.
- Coordinating the development of ROPA for each student, related to the school-based aspects of the course.
- Checking that ROPAs are completed before the end of the practice; agreeing and signing the students' summative statements.
- Before the second placement, examining first school reports and ROPAs to enhance the planning process; checking that targets established in the first practice are being tackled or have been met.
- Formally observing students on the agreed number of occasions and, informally, on any number of occasions.
- Consulting on students' achievements and teaching competence with HEI tutors, subject mentors and other teachers involved in the observation of practice, following the assessment guidelines.
- Where students are in danger of failing the course, alerting them and university staff at an early stage and certainly well before the 'early warning of failure' deadline.

- Compiling a summative report on each student's achievements and competence and, in the case of the final block teaching practice, recommending a pass or a fail.
- Forwarding the summative report to the appropriate person or people by the due date.

The subject mentor

Subject mentors are:

- members of the subject departments which are receiving students;
- experienced and effective teachers;
- open to ideas and willing to examine critically their own practice and that of others through a process of analysis and reflection;
- abreast of developments in their own areas of expertise and of education in general;
- well-versed in departmental policies and procedures;
- supportive of students and exhibiting a positive attitude towards them, while expecting the highest possible standards.

Although the subject mentor is likely to be a named individual, it is important that the whole department is involved through discussions within the department and, where appropriate, through supporting students. A positive attitude towards involvement is essential from all members of the mentoring department. While differences may exist between individual departmental members' practices and views, these differences should enhance, not impair, students' experiences while working in a school.

The subject mentor:

- informs the department of the details and requirements of the scheme (e.g. ROPA) and disseminates university development work;
- maintains contact with the professional mentor and the subject tutor to coordinate the school experience within the department;
- is particularly concerned with the development of students' ability to establish effective practice in the classroom, focusing on subject-specific skills, knowledge and application;
- inducts students into the department and encourages them to become active members of the team as soon as possible;
- acts as students' key 'professional friend' throughout the placement, helping them to integrate successfully into the department and to begin to understand the nature of the job;
- facilitates student self-assessment using ROPA as a focus for professional development;
- assesses the students' teaching competence, in consultation with others involved in the students' practice (e.g. departmental members, the

professional mentor and university tutors) and following the guidelines for assessment.

The subject mentor has responsibility for:

1 The induction of students
   - Providing students with information about the department (e.g. departmental documentation).
   - Introducing members of the department and outlining their roles.
   - Guiding students around the department, focusing on resources available, routines and procedures.
   - Drawing attention to departmental policies and rules (e.g. assessment policy, use of facilities).
   - Outlining expectations about professional involvement as appropriate (e.g. departmental meetings, curriculum development meetings).
   - Providing storage and/or workspace for students (e.g. locker, pigeonhole, desk space).

2 Participation in the school/university programme
   - Liaising over course content with the subject tutor, the professional mentor and the student before and during the placement.
   - Becoming fully aware of the nature of the practice and its place in the course.
   - Organizing a serial practice which has structure and incorporates a variety of activities; for example, observation, seminars and individual work to enable students to move in a planned way from passive to active involvement.
   - Planning a phased introduction to teaching so that students may move smoothly and enthusiastically from the serial practice into the block teaching practice; for example, working with individuals and small groups, assuming responsibility for parts of a lesson, shared lesson planning, team teaching, joint lesson evaluation, shared marking.
   - Building focused observation into the programme accompanied by a full briefing, thorough debriefing and, where appropriate, follow-up work.
   - Focusing the students' attention on pupils' learning and leading their analysis and reflection on practices observed.
   - Arranging a teaching timetable which gives students experience of an appropriate range of ages, ability groups, aspects of the subject, etc.
   - Providing information on groups to be taught, schemes of work, examination syllabi, individual needs, etc.
   - Checking that students' forward plans and lesson preparation are satisfactory for the block practice to begin; in particular, checking that National Curriculum requirements have been understood and are being met.

- Ensuring that students plan in consultation with the colleagues whose lessons they are taking.

3 Contributing to assessment and the completion of ROPA
  - Meeting with individual students to discuss their progress; aiding students in developing self-evaluation techniques and in setting targets for further professional development which address both strengths and weaknesses.
  - Checking that action plans are being implemented and building associated targets into the structured observation of lessons.
  - Negotiating with students regarding the completion of relevant sections of the ROPA.
  - Checking that all ROPAs are completed before the end of the practice and agreeing and signing students' summative statements.
  - Before the second placement, examining first school reports and ROPAs to enhance the planning process; checking that targets established in the first practice are being tackled or have been met.
  - Formally observing students on the agreed number of occasions and, informally, on any number of occasions.
  - Providing a tutorial and a written commentary on all lessons formally observed and, where possible, on sessions observed informally.
  - Informing colleagues about observation and feedback techniques so that the department adopts a consistent approach to working with students.
  - Monitoring each student's progress and keeping the professional mentor informed, especially where difficulties arise.
  - Consulting on students' achievements and teaching competence with HEI tutors, the professional mentor and other teachers involved in the observation of practice, following the assessment guidelines.
  - Where students are experiencing serious difficulties, alerting them and the professional mentor at an early stage and certainly well before the 'early warning of failure' deadline.
  - Contributing to the summative report on each student's achievements and competence and, in the case of the final block teaching practice, recommending a pass or a fail.
  - Carrying out a post-practice tutorial with each student based on the report.

Some practical issues for consideration regarding roles and responsibilities

In Chapter 4, we discuss issues surrounding the selection of mentors. The final section of this chapter highlights *practical* considerations which

mentors regard as key concerns when decisions about roles and responsibilities are being made. Only you are in a position to make the decisions
pertinent to your school and your own situation. Therefore, we make no
attempt to pass judgement on these materials, to offer solutions to dilem-
mas, to resolve contradictions or to make recommendations for 'best'
practice. Best practice in one school might be unworkable in another.
Therefore, the material in this section is offered as a means of raising
awareness of the items which mentors perceive as 'real issues', and as a
stimulus to debate and negotiation. The key issues are remarkably similar
for each group. They are:

- *Rank*: should mentors be 'senior' or 'junior' post-holders?
- *The professional development potential of mentoring*: how and where should
  this be targeted?
- *Mentoring in relation to existing roles and responsibilities*: conflict or com-
  patibility?
- *Time*: the challenge of meeting the time requirements of school-based
  ITE within the resourcing constraints of the school.

Clearly, these issues are rarely experienced in real life as separate enti-
ties. However, for the purposes of analysis and discussion, it is useful to
try to disentangle the different strands. A collection of quotations from the
two groups, presented under the relevant headings, plus a case study
follow for the reader's consideration.

Subject mentors and rank

Being in charge of KS3 Science N.C., I was able to give the student up-
to-date advice on assessment and record-keeping as well as being
aware of the problems of time management in getting everything else
done.

(Subject mentor/second in department)

I naturally have an overview of what's going on in the department,
so I'm in a good position to give that information to the students.

(Subject mentor/head of department)

As head of department with a number of years' experience, I feel I am
in a very good position to support students.

(Subject mentor)

The recent experience as a student teacher followed by a probationary period was invaluable when advising the two students I worked
with.

(Subject mentor/class teacher)

She's not been qualified long herself; I think four years. She's quite young and she knows the problems that we're likely to have and she can warn us about them before they happen, which has been very useful.

(Student teacher)

I think my considerable experience gives the students confidence in me – but the fact that I am not very 'senior' [in terms of promotion] makes me non-threatening.

(Subject mentor / class teacher)

Attention needs to be given to the difficulties of negotiation with more senior members of staff . . . In my position, well, not having any position in the department, I then had to go round the houses via somebody else to get them to say to the head of department what needed to happen and it still didn't happen then and it was very unsatisfactory. I didn't have enough status to be able to say what I wanted to say.

(Subject mentor / class teacher)

Professional mentors and rank

It has enabled me to have a very wide overview of how a school runs and be able to share that with them which, perhaps, somebody else on the staff couldn't have done. As an example, we had a meeting last week when I asked if there were any topics that they wanted to look at . . . and there was a request for an input on LMS [local management of schools]. I'm not sure how many other staff could have picked up that topic and given a broad perspective on how it's changed the school so it's been advantageous in some ways.

(Professional mentor / headteacher)

I think it has to be done at deputy level . . . First and foremost, if you are writing summative reports, you have to have a lot of experience of trainee teachers in a range of disciplines and you have to have curricular knowledge across a wide area when you are drawing together the reports from all the people and putting them into a final report. It implies that kind of experience and that kind of knowledge.

(Professional mentor / deputy headteacher)

The person in the role of professional mentor would need the clout to make things work. We've only had to say the word and it's happened.

(Senior teacher sharing professional mentor role
with another senior teacher)

I think it should be aimed at people like me because I have been a head of department at a previous school and I have got many years' experience, but I haven't got a big sort of job in the school so I haven't got all those sorts of pressures.

(Professional mentor/class teacher)

Mentors and professional development potential

I consulted with them (i.e. heads of department) and we targeted the most likely other person viewing it as a developmental role for a teacher with some experience but some way still to go and some ambition to go on to other things.

(Professional mentor)

Of the four subject mentors, two are youngish people who have visibly benefited from having done this exercise in terms of their ability to collaborate in a group meeting, report-writing and all sorts of things.

(Professional mentor)

We suggest it to people who have got a bit bogged down and need their careers rejuvenating.

(Professional mentor quoted in Fair 1992: 6)

I'm getting towards the latter part of my career and it might otherwise have been easy for me to ease back or slow down or just get stuck in a rut. You're not able to do that when you are working with young teachers. They cause you to reflect upon your present practice and to re-examine it and that is a very helpful thing for anybody at whatever stage of their career they are.

(Professional mentor)

They come, hopefully, with some enthusiasm . . . some new ideas, different ways of looking at things. You know, questioning, 'Why do you do it that way?' 'Because we did it this way for the last ten years'. And you have to justify yourself, so actually that stimulates the department and people like me . . . As far as I was concerned, it kept me awake, it kept me on my toes, got me out of the rut I was in. Actually having to think about why you are doing something and where it is going and that sort of thing, I find very exciting and stimulating . . . It makes me analyse the job a bit more; it makes me sharp.

(Subject mentor)

Time

Over fifty hours of mentoring time was invested in the students and for the students (e.g. in team meetings with the professional mentor and other subject mentors) to ensure all students had an equal and beneficial experience – this time was just for my involvement.

(Subject mentor)

. . . it is clearly the timetable, not some concept of good practice, which is a major determinant of when discussions with the student take place and how effective they may be.

(Professional mentor quoted in Hurst and Wilkin 1992: 53)

. . . most of that time is not in fixed blocks. It's mainly twenty minutes, half an hour here and there, lunch breaks, break times, after school. Some of it is extremely informal but there is a very big time cost.

(Professional mentor)

My subject mentor, although she isn't second in department, is competent for the job. Obviously, the head of department is far too busy to have time.

(Student teacher)

My subject mentor has been very helpful . . . but because he is head of department he has got a lot of other things to think about, so I have tended to discuss things with the second in department or whoever's lesson it is that I'm taking.

(Student teacher)

Huge amounts of time . . . costs to my own preparation just because all my frees have been spent with my students. Every week since the student's been here, I have spent at least two hours a week just talking or going over a lesson. Before the students came, there have been the days of INSET. Just preparing the student timetables took me three hours. I'm sure one gets better at that but it was very time-consuming trying to accommodate everybody. Phone calls in the evening – students ringing me or me ringing students.

(Subject mentor)

An average week does not exist. Students require a greater amount of Professional Mentor time during induction and giving feedback on lessons. At other times, the input is greater from Subject Mentors. It is this imbalance of time which creates difficulties for a Professional Mentor – one or two hours per week is easier to allocate and cover than four or five hours one week and one hour the next week.

(Professional mentor)

Relationship to existing roles and responsibilities

It is quite a useful role for the second in department to have because the head of department is snowed under with other responsibilities, so I can't see anything which is in conflict with my role.

(Subject mentor / second in department)

It's never heads of department . . . definitely not, and they agreed that they should not be mentors. [*Interviewer*: 'Why do you feel it should not be a head of department?'] . . . I think most heads of department, if they are honest with themselves, have got too many other responsibilities . . . They couldn't give the job everything it needs. I've met a lot of heads of department who are doing the job though and they all complain about the question of time.

(Professional mentor)

As an MPG [main professional grade], I am able to concentrate on the responsibilities of mentoring wholeheartedly.

(Subject mentor / class teacher)

We've deliberately not had heads of department doing the job. Heads of department were given the opportunity if they wanted to, but on discussion it was felt that it would be more beneficial to staff who hadn't got any other responsibilities in the school . . . Heads of department have already got quite a lot to do anyway.

(Professional mentor)

I have responsibility for staff professional development and training anyway and therefore the role fits quite well.

(Professional mentor / deputy headteacher)

It also fits in quite well for me as I'm also responsible for NQTs [newly qualified teachers]. Much of the paperwork and routine and the way one operates is similar for both groups. There seems to be a certain logic to my involvement.

(Professional mentor / senior teacher)

My main difficulty, by far, was finding time. The block practice coincided with exams (I am exams officer) and other duties. I shall have more time next year, though I doubt if it will seem like enough. Our overall programme was fine, but I was not happy with my own performance – not enough personal contact with students.

(Professional mentor / senior teacher)

They are usually a lot higher than I am. I noticed at meetings they are nearly all deputies . . . I think research shows that they are the people who do the job least well . . . because it's number fourteen on their list and I think that's quite important.

(Professional mentor / class teacher)

There are certain advantages in having Alan as the professional mentor because he's got less timetabled time that it could actually conflict with, so there are only relatively few occasions when subject mentors have had to be provided with cover to deal with specific items. It's certainly solved the problem of . . . actually working with the group of students.

(Subject mentor commenting on headteacher acting as professional mentor)

Case study: Class teacher acting as professional mentor

The majority of colleagues I have spoken to about teacher education over the past three years have supported the increasing involvement of schools in teacher training – in principle. There are two stumbling blocks, time and money.

Three years ago, our school decided to try an unusual approach which has gone some way to addressing these two issues. When we were invited by a university to take part in a pilot project, the senior management team advertised the role internally as a career development opportunity. They believed in the value of being involved but had no wish to add the title 'professional mentor' to the already long list of responsibilities of a deputy head. No incentive points were offered but there was a small time allowance.

Several members of staff were interested in this avenue of career development and competitive interviews were held. I had recently returned to full-time teaching on the Standard Scale with little opportunity for promotion and I was feeling that my career break, although affording me a variety of breadth of experience, had closed the door to a more challenging or rewarding role. Nevertheless, I was given the post to the surprise of some who had envisaged this as a job only performed by senior teachers. In the first few meetings, surrounded by people with years of school management experience and a cache of responsibility points, my position raised interest, if not eyebrows. Quite a few meetings at the university began with a chairperson asking people to introduce themselves and 'Say what you do'. To answer 'I teach' was a unique response and felt quite daring, almost shocking at first.

It does seem that the idea that only designated managers can handle a professional mentoring role is erroneous. There are many people in classrooms who, for one reason or another, are working without the rewards or responsibility to match their capabilities. Equally, there are many managers who would perform more efficiently unencumbered by such lengthy job descriptions that they rarely have time to draw breath. A whole-school view is desirable in the mentoring role, but it comes with doing the job: it is dependent upon access not status. Luckily for me, I was working in a school where that was acknowledged before it became generally accepted.

I decided to utilize the time allowance available in the form of one school double period per week (1 hour 10 minutes) through the whole year. I could see that the job would take more than an hour each week, but I reasoned that I could give my own time to it when necessary and, when students were not in school, be guaranteed a breathing space.

Accessibility is very important to students – sometimes a high-profile role can make that more difficult to achieve. Students can often see senior staff in offices, leading meetings and dealing with global issues, whereas our mentors' primary task is in the class-room. When I need somewhere private, I will use someone's office; when I need information, I will ask for help or I will delegate or defer to an 'expert'. There is less power to intimidate and less of the 'status' magic that silences children and student alike. Had I been a deputy, however pleasant or approachable, I hardly think a student would have phoned in some distress at 10.30 on a Sunday night to tell me of a 'mistake' she had made on the Friday afternoon. Not only are students less fearful of the ordinary classroom teacher, they also don't see our mentors as being responsible for the whole school, so they tell us more freely what they perceive as needing improvement or what works well or how they feel. There is more of a sense of companionship and support.

I work closely with my line manager who is responsible for staff development, inset and appraisal. This open management structure, with its potential for development and accountability, makes it a viable and, ironically, a high-profile alternative to the traditional model of managing university links.

4 MANAGING MENTORING

Introduction

Effective, efficient and empathetic management of mentoring is an essential ingredient of high-quality, school-based initial teacher education (ITE). In fact, it does not seem unreasonable to suggest that 'success' or 'failure' is totally dependent upon thoughtful and proficient management. On one level, this might seem to be no more than the statement of a commonsense truism. But just as student teachers are encouraged to question all taken-for-granted assumptions and conventional wisdoms, teacher educators should also be concerned to interrogate what is meant by, and what is involved in, commonsense understandings. The aim of this chapter, therefore, is to focus on the management of mentoring for quality provision.

'Quality' is a word that is much bandied about these days. It might be assumed that all providers of ITE are concerned to offer a 'quality' service, but experiences show that, even where this is the aim, it is not always achieved (cf. Reid *et al.* 1994). Quality is an evaluative word, denoting degrees of goodness or excellence. Some people claim that it is possible 'objectively' to assess teacher education in terms of the extent to which, for example, arrangements run smoothly or students demonstrate their mastery of the prescribed competences. However, when we consider that there is by no means general agreement on the purpose of schooling or on how teachers should be educated (or 'trained'), and given the subjective and experiential, interpersonal and situational nature of teaching, the question of what constitutes quality becomes more problematic. What one person considers to be a high-quality placement is the opposite to someone else's view. As one professional mentor put it:

> You know how some people are always on about quality time with their own kids? Well, it seems to me that what I consider quality time with my kids isn't necessarily the same as what you might mean with yours, because we have different interests and concerns and values.

And I think it's the same with teacher ed. I mean, if you're very concerned with the academic side of things, like some teachers I had at
grammar school, and there are some still around, then your 'quality'
teacher training will probably put the emphasis on subject knowledge
and practice in transmission teaching as you might say. If you have a
different philosophy and you work in a school where there aren't the
academic possibilities or interests, then 'quality' preparation has to be
something else entirely. I know these are extremes but you know what
I mean. You can cater for these sorts of differences in school-based
schemes because the student becomes more involved in those particular circumstances, and I think that that's one of their strengths, as
long as you make it clear that it's not always fair or appropriate to
compare what you get in different types of school. In other words,
what's quality here isn't quite the same as what it is somewhere else.

It is not just a question of different interpretations though. Circumstances of various kinds can mean that it is extremely difficult to satisfac-
torily or even adequately meet the various educational and professional
needs of school pupils, student teachers, mentors and other staff in any
particular school. Ensuring that all parties emerge from school-based ITE
programmes having had a positive and worthwhile educational experience on which they can base their future development, i.e. a 'quality'
experience, requires detailed planning and preparation, careful monitoring and critical evaluation. It also demands that everyone should know
what is expected of them. One of the key tasks for those responsible for
managing mentoring is, therefore, establishing and realizing the principle
of whole-school commitment to school-based ITE.

Whole-school commitment

Who decides that a school will be involved in an ITE scheme, and on what
basis do they take that decision? The answer to the first part of the question is in the first instance, usually, if not inevitably, the headteacher
and/or the deputies. In other words, the people responsible for management; those who are, therefore, responsible for managing the ITE. Reasons
for participation are various and complex. For instance, participation in
ITE might be seen as:

- a fundamental professional responsibility to help prepare the next
  generation of teachers;
- a way of bringing in fresh ideas and youthful vitality;
- offering opportunities for various kinds of staff development;
- maintaining a long-standing relationship with a higher education institution (HEI).

In some cases, pragmatic or even material reasons might apply. On occasion, primary headteachers have claimed that their main reason for joining the Open University's teacher education scheme was to get the computer that was part of the deal!

Regardless of who took the initial decision, or of the reasons for involvement, it is desirable that there should be a whole-school commitment to the scheme based on shared understandings both of the role and purpose of ITE and of the roles and responsibilities of the various parties involved. Developing and maintaining that understanding is a crucial and continuing management task. It is not an easy one. Expecting everyone in a staff that may number sixty teachers to be in total agreement about any issue is, perhaps, unrealistic. Indeed, it is just as likely to be unattainable with a staff of four or six. What can be helpful, though, is some sort of statement or policy which sets out what is expected of everyone so that there can be no doubt as to what is required. Specifying what people should actually do is much more likely to succeed than attempting to change attitudes and will probably be much more cost-effective in terms of time and trouble.

Different schools will prefer to develop and draw up their statement at different times depending on how they usually work. Some will do it right at the start, others later, when they have got structures and systems in place. Similarly, different personnel will be involved in the development process. In some schools, statements or policies are drawn up by one person or a small group and are then presented in draft form for discussion and amendment; other staffs involve more people right from the start. Each approach has its merits and drawbacks. You will know what works best in your own circumstances.

The following are two schools' ITE Policy Statements. They are not intended to be read as templates nor as models, but simply as examples.

School 'A': Initial Teacher Education Policy Statement

We recognize that it is healthy for the school to be involved in the training, support and induction of new members of the profession. Teacher education faces an uncertain future; it is in the interests of this school to have clearly established whole-school principles and structures to enable us to respond to changes selectively and productively. Teacher education in this school aims to:

- enable trainee teachers to be an effective resource for children;
- contribute to the quality of teaching and learning within the school;
- enhance professional dialogue with all parties interested in making explicit the connections between theory and practice;

- promote the interest of the school;
- provide a structured introduction to secondary education which fulfils the requirements of training, support and induction.

Trainee teachers are warmly welcomed into the school after wide consultation. This is an ongoing process intended to offer models of good practice and to provide students with sufficient opportunities to develop professional competence.

As a general principle, a third of any funding which accompanies a student will go directly to their subject department. In addition, any department which has to provide materials/resources over and above those which would be used by the classroom teacher can request funding to cover specific resourcing.

However, there are other criteria which would be fairly taken into account:

- the amount/degree of whole-school induction and experience required;
- the nature of the school-based work we are contracted to provide;
- the availability within the department of experienced/interested members of staff to mentor the student;
- the amount of experience the student has;
- any additional benefits provided by the university.

Trainee teachers follow a planned induction programme into school procedures, policies and practices, which will assist their professional development. We place great importance on good personal relationships. Designated mentors are required to be committed and skilled professionals who value students as individuals. Trainee teachers are expected to respect our Ethos Statement and to observe our guidelines on classroom practice. Teaching practice timetables balance, as far as possible, the needs of our pupils, the student and the department. It is expected, and planned, that students will need support and guidance. Negotiated target-setting focuses on specific criteria related to professional competence. Mentors are required to follow stringent procedures for classroom observation, assessment and appraisal of trainee teachers. The school tries to ensure that the training needs of mentors are met. The teacher education provision is regularly evaluated and reviewed to improve the teaching and learning experience and to monitor the costs and benefits to our children and staff.

School B: Teacher Training Policy

The school is committed in principle to *support* initial teacher training; contact with students and college staff is a stimulation to teachers and can bring direct and indirect benefit to the pupils, but care must be taken to ensure that pupils' progress is not adversely affected by excessive exposure to inexperienced recruits to the profession.

1 Our main loyalty in teacher training has traditionally been to X university.

2 We have commonly taken 8–12 students teaching the six most common 'academic' subjects (English, Maths, Science, Languages, History, Geography).

3 The pattern of attachment for students is:
   (a) 12 weeks of induction, observation and preparation in the Autumn term for 2 days/week (Tuesday/Wednesday).
   (b) Full-time teaching practice for the whole of the Spring term and first half of the Summer term.
   (c) Observation in a different school/college for the second half of the Summer term.

4 For each subject an appropriately experienced departmental 'mentor' will be responsible for overseeing the work of the student, ensuring variety of experience and professional evaluation and guidance. There will be some recognition of this in the timetable.

5 The whole programme will be under the supervision of the professional tutor for students, who will liaise with X university and other professional training establishments, work closely with their link tutors, organize a training programme on whole-school issues (Wednesday p.m.) and ensure that proper reports and references are provided. All requests for student attachments should be channelled through the professional tutor who will be responsible for monitoring the effect of student placements on pupils. (Not more than 25 per cent of staff figure in any one year.)

6 Students will be attached to tutor groups and will be encouraged to be involved in all tutor group responsibilities: registers, parental contact, counselling, personal and social education, reviews, as well as residential education and extra-curricular activities.

7 During the Summer term, students complete a dissertation (outside their teaching subjects) linked to their practical experience and observations at the school; the school may seek assistance from them on specific issues and concerns.

8 We would not wish to cause disruption for pupils by taking student teachers in the main subject areas (listed in para. 5) from other teacher training institutions except for observation or as subsidiary subjects. We would welcome, however, placements

for student teachers in other subject areas: Religious Education, Art, Music and Drama, Craft, Design and Technology, Business Studies, Home Economics and Physical Education.

9 We would hope that institutions training teachers in these subjects would be aware of the normal pattern of X university's PGCE students and be willing to fit into a similar pattern of observation or attachments.

10 Supporting student teachers takes teacher time and physical resources. We will need a clear understanding in advance of what proportion of DES funding to colleges is to be allocated to recompense the school for its part in that professional training.

For everyone involved, the mentoring experience needs clarity and coherence. They need to know where ITE fits into the overall work of the school. On a pragmatic level, having documentation ready prepared can alleviate the stress at Ofsted inspection. Such information is important for all participants:

- for the students who have no previous experience of the scheme, but who must be rapidly inducted into it so that they can make the best use of the opportunities presented to them;
- for all teachers, not just those who are involved as designated mentors: all need sufficient knowledge of the scheme to be able to support colleagues and students. They need to be informed about procedures and about such things as lesson observation and feedback techniques, in case students ask to observe them or they are required to observe students. They also need to know what is being done with any monies which may accompany the students. Rumours about money can be pernicious and divisive and are best prevented by open accounting;
- for the senior management team, who need to be sure that the scheme is a positive benefit to the school and who then need to represent this value to governors and parents;
- for the pupils, who need to perceive that being involved with students is a positive rather than a negative experience, and who need to be aware of the important role they play in ITE.

Achieving this coherence is, usually, the responsibility of the professional mentor (see Chapter 3). The professional mentor does not necessarily do all of the work that is involved. Time does, however, need to be allocated for the professional mentor to be able to undertake the role in an effective manner. And indeed, ensuring that everyone with a designated role does, as far as is possible, have the protected time necessary for them to do their jobs is an important and problematic management task. There is no doubt that teachers are hard-pressed to fit everything in. And there are no easy solutions.

Although in Chapter 3 we looked in detail at the roles and responsibilities of the professional mentor, we note here what we consider to be their main functions, namely liaison, planning, information dissemination, evaluation and assessment.

It has been suggested by some practitioners that coherence and cost-effectiveness are best served if a member of the senior management team assumes overall responsibility for ITE, the induction of newly qualified teachers, INSET and appraisal; in other words, that they take global responsibility for initial and continuing professional development. Such an arrangement does not suit all management plans, but where it is felt to be an appropriate approach, it is essential that sufficient time and resources allow the job to be done 'properly'.

We will now pass on to consider the key management task of building the team of people who are to be most closely involved in working with the students – the mentors.

Selecting mentors

Basing ITE in schools puts teachers under considerable pressure to 'get it right'. Their personal professionalism and the future status of teachers in general is at stake and it is important that everyone understands this. If school-based ITE is to be more than a return to a craft-apprenticeship system, which some commentators believe is the intention (e.g. McClure 1993; Barton et al. 1994), then the onus is on all teachers, especially those designated as mentors, to provide a high-quality service. Selecting the 'right' people is crucial and the Office for Standards in Education (Ofsted 1993: 20) requires schools to demonstrate 'clear procedures for the identification of appropriate teachers to be involved in initial training'. Not everyone can, or should, be a mentor. Simply being 'a good teacher' is not enough, for mentoring is not a straightforward extension of being a school-teacher. Different perspectives, abilities, aptitudes, attitudes and skills are necessary, and while 'good teachers' may possess these, it is not inevitable that they will.

Various procedures are available for selecting mentors. Frequently, a personal invitation is made, by senior staff, to people deemed to possess the appropriate characteristics. In these instances, becoming a mentor can be presented and/or be experienced as a professional development opportunity. Advertising the position within the school can, similarly, highlight the role's developmental potential, enhance its status and increase the chances of getting the most suitable person. Far less positive, from all perspectives, are those cases where teachers have been informed, or have even found out, that the designation and the responsibility have simply been added to their written job description: 'It appeared on my job description' (professional mentor); 'I was instructed by the school to take on the role of mentor' (subject mentor).

Pragmatically, of course, there may be little choice when it comes to choosing mentors. At the most basic level, only certain subject departments will be asked to accommodate students (because no HEIs offer courses in the full range of subjects). Factors such as small departments, timetable constraints, examination considerations, personal commitments of staff members, 'political' issues and a variety of practical matters may also narrow the field and result in less than 'ideal' candidates. Where senior staff have very serious reservations, it may be necessary, and professional, for them to withdraw placements. This was the experience of one professional mentor:

> We've had students in the science department ever since the school-based scheme started; then, last year, we had to say 'Sorry. We can't take any scientists'. You see there was a major building programme going on and people were having to plough through a building site every time they went to the labs. That wasn't very good. They also found it was difficult teaching in there because of all the noise and what was going on outside was distracting to the kids. So that was one reason. But the other was that one of our experienced mentors was on maternity leave and another had just left to go elsewhere and to be quite honest with you, I didn't think that the people left were suitable. One was an NQT [newly qualified teacher], one had what you might describe as personality problems – he's a bit curt and not very encouraging I don't think – and then another of them is very dogmatic and not at all inclined to analyse her teaching. Sounds terrible doesn't it? But I didn't think we could offer a very good experience in Science, so I said to the university 'we'll take French and English this year, but not Science'.

Though the roles and responsibilities of subject mentors are examined in Chapter 3, the following characteristics are worth mentioning here. They are offered in the knowledge that they do represent the 'ideal', but this should not prevent them from being the aim. Effective mentors should have experience and expertise in, for example:

- enabling individuals to learn in the ways that are most effective for them;
- ways of managing and organizing classrooms;
- planning and developing curricula;
- matching content and pedagogy to the pupils they teach;
- dealing with difficult pupils;
- a range of marking and assessment, recording and reporting techniques;
- planning and managing practical work, where appropriate;
- working collaboratively with colleagues.

Developing this expertise is a complex and individual process, especially when what is required is that the course produces teachers who are reflective, competent and who have evolved teaching strategies which are appropriate to their own individual characteristics and style. It is not sufficient, therefore, to simply demonstrate how to do something in a particular way. What is required is a more exploratory, discursive process where mentors and students consider particular teaching strategies and skills in detail on the basis of what the student has experienced in the classroom as a teacher, as a member of a collaborative teaching partnership, as an observer or as someone being observed. Of course, such an approach can be cultivated and developed. Probably all mentors could benefit, both in terms of their mentoring responsibilities and with regard to their personal and professional development, from some form of in-service provision. This is often provided by the HEI as an integral part of the ITE scheme, but in other cases it is up to the mentors themselves.

A mentor's personal characteristics and their interpersonal skills and qualities are obviously important (cf. Brooks 1996) as is their professional commitment. In particular, mentors should:

- be enthusiastic about teaching;
- be willing to reflect on their own practice;
- be prepared to examine critically, with students, their own practice;
- be able to articulate their professional knowledge;
- be open-minded with the view that their approach to teaching and learning is not the only one, nor indeed 'the best';
- be willing to develop their own skills in, and understandings of, teaching and learning;
- be accessible, with a sympathetic and understanding approach to students;
- have a positive and encouraging attitude;
- be supportive;
- have the ability to be critical in a constructive manner;
- be a good communicator and a good listener;
- be committed to their role as mentor;
- be aware of relevant educational theories and be able to relate these to their practice.

Awareness of teacher career stages

Over the years, a number of researchers (e.g. Lacey 1977; Connell 1985; Sikes *et al.* 1985; Bullough *et al.* 1991; Furlong and Maynard 1995) have looked at teacher and student teacher socialization and have suggested that there are certain common stages that the majority of teachers pass through. Generally speaking, the models that they posit involve initial idealism, then a period of survival, in which the main concern is to get by or get through. This is followed by a stage in which the teacher feels that they have achieved mastery or at least a basic level of competence. What happens next depends upon contexts, circumstances and personalities; the teacher either rests or works to develop and improve and, perhaps, advance their career. Where the teacher is promoted or moves on to another job, there may be another period of 'survival' followed by mastery, and so it goes on, until a 'coasting', followed by a winding down, withdrawal and pre-retirement stage.

Those with responsibility for selecting mentors, and mentors themselves, are advised to acquaint themselves with the basic pattern of teacher development because, although such models should not be regarded as being definitive, they can be helpful in planning professional development, for they do, at least, give an idea of the sorts of needs and concerns people are likely to have at the various stages of their careers. Such awareness may be particularly pertinent in school-based ITE, because it is other teachers who have the responsibility for socializing newcomers and consequently their attitudes and values are the attitudes and values that the students will have most contact with. As Williams (1993: 409) notes, in school-based ITE, the emphasis is on 'the importance of the student adopting the culture and practices of the school and of the teachers with whom s/he has contact'. This is all very well if the teachers the student works with have 'appropriate' attitudes and values and if they are 'good' teachers, as opposed to simply experienced teachers. The corollary is, however, disturbing. And it is worrying on a less dramatic scale, too, because:

> . . . studies of practice have found that too often trainees' and cooperating teachers' reflections centre superficially on issues such as whether a particular strategy 'worked', on the children's apparent enjoyment of an activity or whether specified objectives had been met . . . in essence focusing on the 'safe' and not the challenging; on the 'existing' and not on the possible.
>
> (Maynard and Furlong 1993: 76)

School-based ITE is, therefore, likely to be more effective and to result in 'better', more reflective teachers if the professional needs of all participants are taken into consideration and are provided for. It may not be meeting a student's needs (or those of the children they will come to teach) if they are placed with someone who is himself 'surviving' or who takes a complacent view of their practice. Having said this, it may be that being asked to act as a mentor can have a positive influence on the motivation and experience of someone who is in a 'coasting' or 'winding down' state of mind. Indeed, it does appear that involvement in ITE can have a revitalizing and professionally beneficial effect for many teachers (HMI 1995; Barker *et al.* 1996). Careful monitoring is clearly essential.

It is important to recognize explicitly that being a mentor can be demanding, especially the first time it is done and particularly if a student is having difficulties. Professional mentors need to think about what support they can offer to mentors who are having a difficult time. While it is an extreme, Jean's experience as a subject mentor serves as an alerting example:

A. was a nightmare. I nearly decided to jack the whole thing in, teaching I mean, because of him. I went home one day and said to my husband, 'I can't take anymore. This is making me ill'. It wasn't just me, everyone who had anything to do with him got totally stressed out. His university tutor actually got alopecia, which her doctor told her was stress-related and she put it down to A. Anyway, my husband said, 'Don't be daft. You're a head of department, you've got nearly 20 years experience and you're letting him do this to you'. I mean he was right but A. was so awful. His attitude was so pompous and superior, he thought we did everything wrong and he told the kids that as well. He couldn't control his classes and he rubbished the kids left, right and centre. I know that our catchment isn't the best, but it's not the worst either, and one day he came out with 'I don't know how you've got any self-respect working here'. You couldn't tell him anything. I spent hours going over his lessons and I gave him resources and God knows what. The only way I managed to get through was because Tom, the professional mentor, was always ready to let me go and off-load to him. And A. was giving him a hard time too. It was really funny at times. There'd be me, Tom and Pam, the university tutor, and we'd sit there talking about how we could support and help A. when he was doing us all in! We needed the support!

Building a team

All mentors and mentoring departments should be aware of what is expected of them well before any students arrive in the school. One way of doing this is to communicate directly with each mentor, but this means wasting the opportunity to develop a team approach to the scheme. A team approach has staff development potential and it can also help to make the professional mentor's task less onerous. As was noted earlier, a whole-school commitment to ITE is desirable: if subject mentors share perceptions of their roles and responsibilities, of the aims and objectives of the scheme, and of likely difficulties, problems may be avoided. For instance, students placed within the same school, but in different departments, inevitably compare how they are treated and the provision that is made for them. Sometimes differences are appropriate: students have different needs and they don't all progress at the same rate. It is also true that different subjects make different demands on teachers, and students learning to teach them need different levels of support. For instance, practical work, in Science or Physical Education, raises issues to do with safety, making it necessary for mentors to accompany students for longer than is the case in other subject areas. In other cases, though, and with regard to such details as how students are introduced to pupils, student access to, and guaranteed contact time with, their mentors, and access to resources such as photocopying and room keys, differential treatment is less easily justified. Having a whole-school approach, possibly based on a written student teacher 'entitlement' document, can help to protect students, pupils and mentors alike. Below, in an example which points to bad practice, a subject mentor explains how she found out about how a mentor in another department dealt with his student.

I've been doing an MA and my dissertation was a case study of school-based ITE in my school. I interviewed a subject mentor in another department, her student and the professional mentor. It was quite disturbing really, because I knew from talking to Kay that what they did in the English Department was pretty similar to us in Modern Languages. I don't see the Science people though because they tend to stay in the department, so I didn't know but I assumed that things were similar there too. When I interviewed the student she was ever so pleased with how she was being treated, especially as at her first school her mentor hadn't been very good at all. And I knew Kay and that she was really, really professional and an excellent teacher and very committed, so I wasn't surprised, but then the student started talking about the boy in the Science Department and what a bad time he was having because his mentor wasn't at all helpful, didn't observe him, couldn't be bothered to look at his plans and then when he did come in, he'd be negative and critical and didn't offer constructive advice. And I didn't know what to do because I was doing this research, under a confidential thing, and yet I was a mentor in the school, so I really didn't know what to do, and it was so unfair in my opinion.

Experience, and the above example, shows that being a 'lone' mentor within a department is not ideal. A group of colleagues working with students not only shares the load but also provides a range of experience and expertise which is valuable to the team as well as to the student. An important benefit of having students in school is that they can provide the impetus – and the opportunity for members of a department, or a group of teachers more generally – to reflect critically on, and to examine, their

own practice. On these grounds, many schools have encouraged departments to take on a group responsibility for mentoring, with the designated
subject mentor acting as coordinator.

> How we've worked it is so that Bri is the subject mentor in title but
> the students come into all our classes, or as it seems appropriate. If
> you're just with one person all the time, you don't get to see different
> approaches and styles and you don't get the range of classes. In any
> case you find that you get on better with some people than you do
> with others, so in that sense it protects the student a bit more – and it
> protects us because you can get students that you don't find it com-
> fortable to work with.
>
> (Teacher)

> Nicky was very volatile. She got this idea that Lyn, her mentor, had
> it in for her because she didn't like Nicky's attitude and her way with
> the class. It got quite unpleasant at times because she'd spoken to her
> tutor at the university and she came in once or twice to try and sort
> things out. I felt sorry for her because she only had Nicky's side of
> things and she was inclined to accept that, but there wasn't much she
> could do really, not actually being here. It was a personality thing
> really. The only way we managed it was by me and Sara taking more
> responsibility for Nicky and that worked much better. We decided
> then that this was how we'd work in future, with us sharing students
> as it were.
>
> (Teacher)

All departments, regardless of size, contain teachers with a range of
teaching styles. This is both a strength and a weakness as far as mentoring is concerned: working with a range of styles is important for students
but they do need to understand why different people develop and use
different styles. This is an issue which needs to be addressed fairly early
on.

If a department is to take on group responsibility for mentoring, the
subject mentor's role becomes one of coordinating the department's work
with the student as well as dealing directly with them. Some schools
appoint heads of department as subject mentors, feeling that this fits well
with the other responsibilities of the post. Others feel that the head of
department already has enough to do and that this is an opportunity for
staff development; they consequently offer the job to another member of
the department. And in some cases, departments appoint more than one
subject mentor.

However, there are potential difficulties if a whole department takes on
the responsibility for mentoring. There may be times when students and
teachers have different perceptions of the department and its work. A cosy

and well-knit department seen from the outside may seem complacent and unfriendly. Rightly or wrongly students assigned to such departments may feel like intruders. Alternatively, or at the same time, they may find it difficult to 'escape' from the department and gain wider, whole-school experience. Everyone who has ever worked in a secondary school knows just how territorial and insular some departments can be:

> We are a very tight-knit department and I don't think that's unusual. You go to many, if not most, schools and there's the PE Department, the craft people and the scientists and they spend most of their time in the department. They have their coffee there and do their preparation there and generally stay together. And this usually is because they've got what they need there: if you're a practical subject, then your stuff's there and the other thing, of course, is that they've got the prep rooms or the stock room and the space and it just seems more convenient to stay around. When I was a student I didn't even know where the staffroom was, no-one went there. And that wasn't good. But I didn't see it then. It's only since I've got into a job where there is a managerial role and where you're not just concerned with teaching your subject to kids, that you really see it, at least it was for me. I mean you get aware of what other people think about you and how this affects how they regard you and how they behave towards you. And you get to find things out if you mix more. You find out about kids and who's doing what and why. Things have changed. There is much more whole-school initiative going on these days, because there are whole-school policies on things like homework and equal opportunities and discipline and that stops you being so insular, but now I'm a mentor one of the first things I say is, 'Do you want to be a stereotypical science teacher? Because if you do, stay in the department, never go across to the staffroom but I don't recommend it.' I make a point of always spending at least some time everyday in the main staffroom and I try and encourage my staff to, and I definitely advise the students to. I think it's in everyone's interests in the end, and it's in the kids' interest as much as anything.
>
> (Subject mentor)

It is possible that involvement in student mentoring may lead to positive changes in this area of school life:

> There are a lot of benefits for the institution hopefully. For example, I can think of one thing at the moment where there is one particular faculty who tend to spirit their PGCE students away a little and we are working very hard towards drawing the students back into the main school in the hope that, in fact, that will encourage the rest of the staff to come back in, and certainly the renewed emphasis on

communication between the ITT coordinator and the mentors this year, I hope, will encourage much more sharing of students' ideas and within the college . . . I want to see it grow a lot more and I think it will.

(Professional mentor)

Within a department, colleagues may have different perceptions of students who are struggling or who seem to need more help than others. It is easy to write-off students if they are having difficulties, particularly if confident and competent students are paired with them. Where this happens there needs to be consideration, both of the student's perceived difficulties and of the assumptions and underlying views of teaching, mentoring and the role of HEI staff, which give rise to such perceptions. These and related issues need to be considered by the department. Dealing with problems such as these is best done through the provision of regular, scheduled meetings and, once again, if it is approached in the 'right' way, these can serve as a vehicle for staff development.

The team approach to mentoring results in an organizational structure which, within a school where there are students in a number of departments, can be represented schematically as in Fig. 3. This structure has the benefit of creating discrete teams, each of which can be managed separately on a day-to-day basis by the professional and subject mentors. However, where such a structure is adopted, it will be important to ensure that:

- communications reach everyone;
- having departmental groups does not damage the coherence of the scheme as a whole;
- there are opportunities for everyone involved to get together.

Research has shown considerable variation in the time which schools provide for mentoring. While some mentors have two or more hours each week designated for the task, others have none (Barker *et al.* 1996). Good practice which exists in this area needs to become widespread. Mentoring responsibilities should be matched with a suitable time allocation. Although mentors rarely find the time that they have available adequate for the size of the job, it is important that there is at least one guaranteed period each week which is set aside exclusively for the purpose.

Having established a mentoring team, the next stage is for team members to work together on developing their own scheme, bearing in mind any pre-existing requirements and/or terms of reference agreed between the HEI and participating schools. Before any students arrive in the school, meetings will be necessary to ensure that everyone knows exactly what is expected of them. If people cannot attend any of these meetings, then it is essential that they receive detailed communications. In

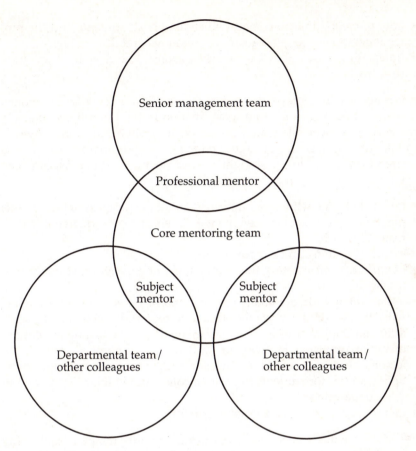

Fig. 3 Organizing a team approach to mentoring.

a successful mentoring scheme, no assumptions of awareness or knowledge are ever made. This means that any new mentors are fully inducted, preferably by the professional mentor.

Team meetings

It is likely that initial team meetings will focus on aims, roles, responsibilities and practical issues, such as making time for mentoring work. Indeed, time management and timetabling issues should be a priority both at whole-school and departmental level. In all schools there is a need to discuss such matters as:

• whether 'protecting' certain year groups from students, because of examinations, leads to other groups being 'over-exposed', and, if so, what should be done about it;

- how to create timetable space which allows all students and the professional mentor to get together for seminars and discussions;
- timetabling which allows feedback sessions to be close to observation sessions.

It is also useful to develop a policy on what is to happen to any money that the school may earn from participation in the ITE scheme after the mentoring has been adequately resourced and, where appropriate, who is to take up any training or higher education opportunities that may be offered in addition to the straightforward payment. Other issues which need to be discussed at an early stage include:

- how to keep the whole staff informed about the progress of the scheme;
- maintaining contact between mentors to encourage and strengthen the team approach;
- mentors' training and support needs;
- identifying and meeting the expectations of colleagues, students and teachers;
- letting mentors know about any research or other kinds of academic work that the HEI expects the student to undertake while in school;
- a unified approach to basic requirements (e.g. establishing an 'entitlement' of provision in terms of such things as number of observed lessons, student access to resources including work and storage space, opportunities for students to observe colleagues in their 'home' and in other departments);
- giving feedback and constructive criticism.

The team will also need to meet during and after the practice. During the practice, meetings will be useful for reviewing student progress and identifying strategies to deal with any situations which have arisen. At the end of the practice, it will be important to undertake a review, or evaluation, as a basis for future planning. This should involve students.

Of course, the main function of team meetings is to keep people up-to-date with everything that is going on. On occasion, and if possible, it may be appropriate to invite HEI staff along to share information, to talk about their roles and their expectations of the students and the school, and to discuss quality assurance issues. Such meetings can do much to foster a sense of partnership and get away from the 'us and them' attitude which can exist on both sides.

Collecting and disseminating information

Convening meetings is one aspect of the responsibility for collecting and disseminating information which forms a crucial part of the professional mentor's job. He or she needs to be the first person to whom colleagues can turn if they require information about the scheme, so it is important that they should have an easy and efficient reference system. Experienced professional mentors have found that it is useful to have a reference file where all information relating to the scheme is held. It is a good idea to make this file accessible, at all times, to anyone who may need to use it, so it should be kept in the school office, the staffroom or library. Such a file is only useful if it contains up-to-date and relevant information. Maintaining it is another task for the professional mentor.

The reference file should contain, as a minimum, details about:

- the structure of the students' course, with information about the higher-education-based component and details of any research assignments students may be working on while in school;
- dates and deadlines for the school and for the students (e.g. when 'concerns' about student performance have to be reported, when reports need to be returned, assignments handed in, etc.);
- names and telephone numbers of higher education contacts;
- the names of students, with details of their subjects and interests as well as any special needs (if possible, it is a good idea to include a photograph);
- specimens of any forms associated with the practice, together with notes on their completion;
- a list of any regulations relating to the scheme (e.g. DfE competences);
- the school's policy on student teachers;
- a 'survival pack' for students.

Some of these details may be contained in documents issued by the HEI, by the DfE, Ofsted and so on. Other information will be collected from the students themselves.

The following is a contents page from one school's reference file:

Teaching practice file

Contents

Section 1: Official documentation
    University's school partnership handbook
    Record of professional achievement
    9/92 competencies
    School policy on teacher education
    University observation sheets
    University course subject booklets
    University professional studies booklets

Section 2: School documentation
   List of subject mentors
   Timetable for teaching practice
   List of teachers and groups involved
   Focused observation sheets
   Observation report forms
   Summative report forms

Section 3: Students
   Students' CVs
   Reports from previous placements

Another useful strategy is to have a year planner devoted to ITE pinned up on some easily accessible wall. As well as showing key dates, this can also contain important names and telephone numbers.

We have already noted the need for regular meetings to keep members of the mentoring team up-to-date and to provide mutual support. Such meetings are likely to be the most effective and efficient way of disseminating and collecting information. Information about students is likely to come from two main sources: from the HEI and from the students themselves. In many schemes, students are asked to complete curricula vitae (CVs) which are then sent to their placement schools. Where these exist they should be circulated to each member of staff who has responsibility for the student. If such an arrangement is not built in to the scheme, then schools could request CVs either before students come into school, or on their initial visit.

If the student has already completed one practice, then it will be important to gather some information from their first school. Reports are often passed on as a matter of routine, but where this does not happen it is useful to get hold of them. These reports provide valuable information about the student which can help in planning for their practice. However, it is important to remember that schools have different philosophies and departments are run in different ways. Students may find it hard to adjust from one department to another and may rush into mistaken judgements unless this issue is specifically prepared for and addressed. It is also very unhelpful for students to get informal messages from teachers that school B is going to be difficult, for whatever reason, compared to school A. Professional mentors should be on guard for instances of negative gossip-mongering and should ensure that students are advised to take what they hear about other schools with a pinch of salt.

As well as providing information about the practice and the student for teachers in the school, it is a good idea to compile a reference file or 'survival package', which deals with life in the school, for the student. Such a package might include:

- a copy of the staff handbook;
- school aims;
- discipline procedures and available sanctions;
- who to consult if pupils present with various problems;
- details about coffee/lunch;
- where to park cars;
- how to get materials photocopied;
- how to address the headteacher;
- what is considered acceptable dress and appearance for teachers at the school (e.g. are jeans and nose rings acceptable?);
- notification procedures in case of absence;
- equal opportunities policies;
- access to resources, including information technology (IT).

Each school has its own idiosyncrasies. In some schools, it is acceptable for teachers to sit in the staffroom and read the paper or knit or chat. In others, such behaviour is seen as indicative of laziness. And people have different expectations for students and teachers. For example:

> Some members of staff did comment to me that Scott was sitting in the staffroom reading a science fiction novel during free periods. This didn't go down very well because they thought that he shouldn't be doing that, that he ought to be spending all his time preparing lessons. I told him this and he was quite surprised and a bit upset because he felt that he'd done his preparation at home in his free time and he was just sort of trading that, but I told him that it wouldn't do for him to be seen doing nothing if he wanted to get a good report.
>
> (Professional mentor)

> Di [the professional mentor] more or less told me off for sitting in the staffroom reading a book. She said that people had been complaining to her about it because they said I wasn't behaving like a teacher and I clearly wasn't doing the proper preparation. I thought, 'get a life!'. I'd been up to three o'clock that morning preparing bloody lessons and I felt that I deserved a rest. I think it's pathetic because they'd made these assumptions and gone off to Di when they should have asked me. I can't stand that petty attitude.
>
> (Student)

Students need to be told about things like this. They cannot be expected to know and, furthermore, they may have experienced a very different climate in another school. It is also the case that in some staffrooms people still have their 'own' chairs, or their own mugs, and students need to be warned about this. It might sound a small thing, but 'upsetting' someone by drinking out of their cup can, in a student's eyes, influence their entire practice.

They've got this coffee bar and a woman comes in to make the tea at breaks. And the first day, I went for a coffee and paid the money and just picked up this mug and nobody said anything. And the same thing happened at the next break and somebody said, all snidey like, 'Are you working your way through all the staff mugs then?' And it turns out they've all got their mugs and woe betide you if you use the wrong one. But what got me was that no-one told me and the person whose mug I'd used must've sat there getting cross and didn't say anything. It would have been better if they'd said and I'd have known then, but as it was I felt really embarrassed and stupid and I resent that, feeling that over a mug. And I thought God, if that's your attitude to that, then what's it like to other things? Talk about smallminded.

(Student)

Planning the programme

Like all teaching and learning experiences, school practices need to be carefully planned and matched to students' needs. Before starting to plan in detail, it is a good idea to run through the aims of the programme. While these may vary slightly from scheme to scheme, there are some fundamental points and it is these that we now discuss.

The programme needs to complement other learning from other parts of the entire course. It is a mistake to conceive of and view it as something discrete that happens within a specific school. Usually the HEI will, through documents, personal contacts, meetings and training sessions, emphasize and demonstrate that any programme is part of a whole and will make the links clear. School/HEITE is, ideally, a partnership to which each partner makes their own special and unique, but well coordinated contribution, though sometimes this point seems to be forgotten.

Each scheme may make its own suggestions as to what is to be included in the students' programme, but generally the aims of being in school are:

- to provide teaching experience;
- to allow students to gain and develop the prescribed competences;
- to provide opportunities for guided reflection on students' teaching;
- for experienced practitioners to observe and give students feedback on their practice;
- to introduce students to wider aspects of schooling and teaching than just teaching their subject;
- to allow students to experience the professional culture within a school;
- to provide a context to which students can relate their theoretical learning;

- to give students access to information/opportunities for research necessary to allow them to complete assignments set by the HEI;
- to create staff development opportunities for teachers in school.

Clearly, the specific and unique contribution that schools can make to ITE is practical experience and access to the expertise and knowledge of experienced practitioners. By and large this is provided through a programme of:

- focused/directed classroom observation;
- collaborative teaching;
- individual teaching;
- timetabled reflection and feedback;
- seminars and workshops dealing with specific aspects of schooling, the education system and professional concerns.

Mentors need to devise a programme for each student which provides a varied experience in terms of different age ranges, different abilities and temperaments, different syllabi and different teaching styles. As was noted previously, pragmatic concerns can intrude and make selecting such a variety difficult or even impossible. To some extent, mentors have to make the best of the resources they have to hand, but once again there is no harm in aiming for the ideal.

As with all teaching programmes, it is important to be flexible and to modify plans when and where it may prove necessary. Student teachers, like other learners, come with a range of experiences, have different needs and progress at different rates, and their individual programmes should be constructed with this in mind and in consultation with them. At this point, it is worth remembering that students may themselves have contributions to make in terms of knowledge and expertise. Devising a programme should not be regarded simply as a one-way transaction if everyone is to benefit to the full extent, in professional, educational and in more pragmatic terms:

> We found out, quite by chance actually, someone saw her in a race one Sunday morning, that Sue was a keen cyclist. We didn't have a cycling club but we asked her if she'd be interested in helping set one up and she did and she came back when her course was finished and really put a lot of time and effort in to it and it's thriving now, all thanks to her.
>
> (Professional mentor)

> Well, Rog wasn't the most effective of teachers in the classroom but he got on really well with the staff – because he was older he was more used to the work environment and, I feel a bit guilty about this really, he had fund-raising skills from his previous career and we milked

him for all he was worth, picking his brains and getting him doing things. It was him who really got us going with sponsorship deals if truth be known. The school benefited enormously.

(Subject mentor)

Also, progression is important and students at different points in their course require different programmes. There is little point in giving a second placement student the same timetable as someone on their first placement. Once again, it comes back to getting to know the students and induction programmes should be planned with this in mind.

The induction itself will be the time when students and teachers in school will form their crucial first impressions of each other. It is vital, therefore, that the experience is as positive as it can be for everyone involved. Students need basic information about the school, of the kind mentioned earlier when we were discussing a student's survival package. While much of this can be conveyed through documentation, it will also be important to talk students through it, touching on significant, specific or pressing items. During their first few days in school, students are likely to be bombarded with information, so although it is important to provide written details for later reflection and reference, it is worth remembering that there is nothing more daunting than being confronted with a heap of papers. At this stage, information is, perhaps, most usefully conveyed on a 'need to know' basis, although this requires careful monitoring to ensure that needs are kept satisfied.

During the induction period, there are a number of specific points which must be established between the student and the school. These include:

- the student's timetable. Clearly, it will not be possible to negotiate all aspects of the timetable, but there should be some opportunity for the students to state their preferences. In addition, students may wish to get involved in extracurricular activities or to look at areas such as special needs, IT, or equal opportunities policies. It is important to try and plan for this as well as for classroom teaching. One general aim of giving schools greater involvement in ITE is that students should experience the culture of the school;
- the objectives of the practice. It is important that the students and the school are clear about what competences they are working towards during the placement;
- the assessment and reporting of the practice. Assessment of one form or another will be taking place during the course of the practice and will obviously be of great significance for the student. It is important, therefore, to provide opportunities to work collaboratively with students and colleagues to ensure that assessment is consistent and effective;
- the nature of the involvement of other staff and institutions;

- the purpose, pattern and nature of observations by both students and staff. Where possible, this should be agreed in advance and only varied as a result of discussion between the parties involved;
- specific targets for the students and the school. These can be drawn up during the initial stages of a student's attachment and can serve as a measure of performance and progress.

When the school placement falls close to the start of a student's course, it is unwise to assume that they have any experience of teaching. It is sensible, therefore, to start with a focus on enabling students to understand the basics of teaching and also to gain a sense of what it is like to be in a school as a teacher. It is important that everyone involved understands this. Establishing realistic expectations – of teachers as well as students – is important and may require pre-practice meetings. It also requires that school staff are familiar with what the students have been doing in the higher-education-based component of their course. Once the students are in school, specific programmes can then be tailored to meet their particular needs.

Later, if placements fall in the Spring and Summer terms, it is still unwise to assume too much. There should, of course, be more information available, in the form of reports from first practices and from the HEI, but matching students to provision is still the order of the day. Earlier we noted that each school is different. When they come to their second placement, students will have ideas that are firmly rooted in the school where they have had most of their teaching experience to date. This can cause problems if students' expectations and experiences are not explored and made explicit.

Ongoing review

Throughout the operation of the scheme, there needs to be constant review and reflection. Questions which could guide this include:

- How do student teachers/mentors/pupils/other members of staff experience our ITE provision?
- What are our aims?
- Are these appropriate in our context?
- What do we need to do to achieve them?
- Are we doing these things?
- How will we know if we are 'succeeding'?
- Are there alternative approaches?
- Have we chosen the best approach?
- What evidence do we have to suggest that are succeeding?
- How can we improve provision?

This is not an exhaustive list. The important thing is to review in the specific context and to seek the views of everyone concerned. It takes time, but the process of review is not only a means of assessing how the scheme is progressing, and of identifying ways of refining and improving it, but is also a vehicle for staff development, in that it invites professional reflection and discussion. In Chapter 7, we will look at ways in which school-based ITE can make a significant contribution to staff development.

Managing mentoring is a difficult task because it involves meeting the needs of so many different people – students, teachers, pupils. Constant review and reflection are essential if things are to work smoothly. At the end of this section, we offer two case studies which look at aspects of managing mentoring.

Case study: Dealing with more than one institution of teacher education

Like many schools, over the years we have built relationships with several universities offering a variety of subject specialisms which the implementation of Circular 9/92 caused us to re-evaluate. Education courses in some subjects actually closed, others were being introduced. Some partnerships looked more attractive than others but asked for a greater commitment. We had to look carefully at terms and contracts but decided that, as far as possible, we would try to continue offering a range of placements in the interests of preserving and developing the quality of teaching and learning.

This year, as teacher education coordinator, I have negotiated with ten heads of department about their needs and their department's ability to offer students a quality experience. We do not necessarily use the same departments each year. Sometimes, departments feel particularly under pressure and welcome a break and sometimes students are eagerly sought by departments who previously had none. Dealing with more than one university gives us this flexibility, spreads the burden and affords more staff mentoring experience. This year we will have provided placements for students from six universities. While our commitment has been made in our best interests, facilitating cross-curricular cooperation and a healthy sharing of experience, there are difficulties in dealing with so many institutions.

The documentation, although all mindful of DfE Circular 9/92, varies considerably, not only in terms of amount and clarity, but also in its practical implications. One university's end of practice assessment asks for all competences, including those under the heading 'Potential for further professional development', to be graded and a humble, formal observation sheet, of which there

must be three per student, requires nineteen grades from A to E
plus comments. This is vastly different to the prose descriptions
welcomed by other institutions. In addition, the emphasis placed on
assessment by negotiation between student and mentor, or the role
of action-planning, varies in degree as well as in methods of recording. The payment, and the procedure for payment, also varies.
Some calculate funding by the day, some by the number of practices, some favour 'base' or 'principal' schools and, perhaps more
importantly, one institution requires us to invoice their finance
department a week or two before the students leave – most do not
require us to invoice them at all.

Quite early on it became apparent that, regardless of the wealth
or welter of documentation, we needed a school policy on teacher
education and that it should be written in the language of our
school aims and ethos, particular to our own school culture. It
would set down clear principles by which we could manage the
partnerships and would be available to all interested parties – staff,
parents, governors, universities and inspectors. To this original
policy we have added other documentation, for example written
criteria for the allocation of the disparate funding which comes into
the school. We found that different areas of the curriculum, not to
mention individuals, bore different costs.

All the universities I have dealt with are trying to involve
teachers in the planning process. Involvement necessitates meetings. In my experience, colleagues in further education are well
aware of the problems and try to accommodate schools. Although
the meetings convened by the institutions often cover the same
theoretical ground, they take differing philosophical stances and
this understanding and the chance to share perceptions with colleagues is invaluable in running the scheme sensitively and
smoothly. In practice, we have to limit time out of school. I have
found that often a member of staff has more frequent contact with a
particular establishment, or interest in a specific area, and I encourage that and rely on those links.

We try to balance number and times of teaching practices so that
our children and staff are not overburdened and so that students
receive from us the quality of experience they deserve. The timings
of the practices are difficult to cater for in the school timetable, particularly to free someone with a heavy teaching load to lead serial
practice sessions when institutions use different days of the week:
there is less costs, and less time taken, in talking to eight students
at once than in talking to four groups of two. We do as much pre-
planning as possible, using a variety of staff, on a rota system for
induction sessions. I plot all practices and assessment dates on a

year planner, including any details of assignments that universities ask their students to complete while with us. We then try to run sessions concurrently with newly qualified staff, or tie up, for example, a student's assignment on differentiation with a practical workshop in the special needs department. As far as possible, we give students real tasks. Tracking and observation can, for example, supply pastoral managers with insights into pupil behaviour obtained by students.

Although it is not a substitute for dialogue, I find we have to have a *Student Handbook*. It is, in part, the *Staff Handbook*, but much slimmed down to include those things that students will find useful and, as time goes by, we personalize it, adding things that we have used, such as 'How to write a worksheet' (complete with graphics), and it includes my home telephone number for emergencies – used only once, but wisely in three years. With so many students, in a large, split-site school, I feel it important to maximize accessibility and to have at least some quality control of information.

Similarly, constantly changing teams of mentors need access to information and resources beyond rushed meetings and scribbled notes. I file a copy of all information given to mentors in large ring-binders, labelled with the relevant university and make these accessible to mentors in the staffroom. Mentoring resources are collected and made available, often in conjunction with materials pertaining to appraisal, where we find considerable overlap, and we try to use all available career development opportunities offered by the mentoring experience.

More universities equals more visits to the school. Those from lecturers keen to 'get stuck in' are very welcome, but especially noteworthy are the visits from Ofsted inspectors inspecting teacher education courses. Their demands are not particularly excessive on their visits to partnership schools, but they do tie up at least the students and their mentors, as well as the professional mentor, for at least half a day, in addition to the time taken to prepare for their visit. 'Just briefly', said an Ofsted inspector, pencil poised, 'as you deal with several universities, would you tell me how you moderate the assessment of competences?'

Case study: Time management

Time management in any organization is a difficult thing to get right. Schools are a particular case in point because time is much more tightly controlled – everyone is on a timetable and time throughout any typical day is allotted for the various tasks that have to be done. However, most teachers would claim these days that there is not sufficient time for all the out-of-class activities: marking, preparation, meetings, courses and so on. Add in the complexity of two or more students on teaching practice and suddenly the very small amount of time that most teachers have as 'free periods' becomes even smaller.

When we first entered the mentoring scheme, a lot of questions were asked about the amount of time it would take and how the scheme would be managed. Whose time would be involved? Over what sort of period? Was the new system going to be different and more demanding compared to the old teaching practice where the university had a far greater input? Luckily, our previous experience of students on teaching practice informed our understanding of some of the problems that inevitably arise when two new 'members of staff' arrive on the doorstep on Monday morning and have to be looked after for the next six weeks.

Unless the school is geared up for the visit, there is a tendency to forget about students arriving on the first day. In the first year of the scheme, we failed to ensure that we knew who was coming and who they should see on their first day – the process was thrown into utter confusion. Subsequently, we have paid more attention to pre-planning, ensuring that the right person is in the right place and that the appropriate amount of time is set aside to deal with students on the first day. Further, we ensure that students' timetables are finalized well before the students' visit – this has implications for the teachers whose classes will be taken by students and the subject mentor who has to look after them. The first few days are very costly in terms of time.

It soon became apparent that there are two areas of time management that need to be considered: for staff and for the students. Part of our induction process involves teaching students to manage their time effectively, which includes:

- lesson planning and the management of time in the classroom;
- 'free time' planning – what to do with the 50 per cent of the week that they are not teaching;
- planning time to keep TP [teaching practice] files up-to-date and to evaluate lessons;
- planning time when at home to avoid students' 'burning out' within the first week.

For the mentor, planning time when the practice is under way is crucial, especially daily or weekly meetings with the students. I make it my practice to meet formally with the students once a week, but to talk informally to them every day. Other members of staff must be brought into the process, too, particularly within the faculty team. Those members of staff will have to give time to the students – observing lessons, discussing lesson plans, dealing with problems in the classroom, helping with resources and so on. Delegation is essential for the mentor, because within the tightly structured day of a school, it is not possible to do everything oneself, especially when there are the mentor's own classes to teach as well!

So far under the new scheme, we have been lucky in the quality of the students who have come to us. But, however good they are, they will still need support and guidance at times, especially if they have a particularly difficult class or pupil. Counselling sessions with distraught students can be massively expensive in terms of time, often the problem having to be dealt with then and there. What might be routine to a seasoned pro in dealing with problem pupils can be quite traumatic for the novice who tends to become more involved with pupils than an experienced teacher who knows when to step back and maintain professional distance.

Unfortunately, these sessions can almost never be planned for, but they might take the mentor away from his or her own class and the knock-on effect has to be borne by colleagues. However, the need for such sessions can be anticipated and should be kept in mind when rescheduling the mentor's timetable.

Most exercises in time management are designed to allow you to maximize your time and to use it in the most effective manner. In a profession where time is at a premium and there is never enough of it, my experience of being a subject mentor is that having students inevitably means that there is even less. This is true also for the professional mentor and the subject teachers whose lessons are taken by students.

From my experience, these are the things which I feel need to be taken into account when planning the time budget for hosting students on teaching practice:

For the subject mentor
- pre-practice meetings
- the induction process
- preparing the students' timetable
- meeting with colleagues who will be involved
- observations of lesson
- 'fire-fighting' and trouble-shooting

For the professional mentor
- initial planning meetings with subject mentors
- meetings with students
- meetings with subject mentors during the practice
- contact with university tutors
- informal meetings with students and colleagues

- counselling
- planning meetings with students and staff
- ROPA [record of professional achievement] interviews
- writing reports
- informal meetings with students and colleagues
- contact with university tutors
- training sessions for staff

- report writing/administration of the scheme
- training sessions for colleagues

For the students
- lesson planning
- evaluation sessions
- meeting with professional/subject mentors
- fact-finding about the school
- work on teaching practice files
- consultation with university tutors
- other demands of the university

Much depends upon pre-planning and prioritizing. Although specific problems cannot be predicted, they can be anticipated, which makes it easier to deal with them when they do arise.

5 WORKING WITH STUDENTS

Introduction

We all know the saying that goes, 'Those who can, do, those who can't teach, and those who can't teach, teach teachers'. Everyone involved in education knows that this is rubbish, although that hasn't stopped us from feeling irritated by it. We know full well, and can demonstrate, that what we're about is very much concerned with 'doing', and the advent of school-based initial teacher education (ITE) makes this even clearer. But 'doing', by itself, is not enough and we need to ensure that we don't leave it at that. As Peter Tomlinson (1995: ix) warns:

> What school-based teacher preparation gains by way of relevance, it may lose by way of unreflective narrowness, not to mention lack of effectiveness even at the instrumental level of teaching, since for teaching to be effective, it must at least be intelligently skilful.

In this chapter, we focus on ways in which mentors can work with student teachers to help them become competent and reflective practitioners. In other words, to help them to 'do', and to know why they 'do' it. Once again we wish to emphasize that we see school-based ITE as a partnership between schools and higher education institutions (HEIs), with each partner contributing what they are best at. As Hagger *et al.* (1993: 9) point out, 'there is no reason to believe that schools are well placed to do the work that was previously done by the colleges as well as the colleges themselves do it'. Hence the key questions have to be:

- what can students experience and learn in school that they can't learn elsewhere?
- what can mentors in schools provide that higher education staff can't?

On the view that we are taking, the answers are that schools provide experience of, and practical learning opportunities within, a specific professional environment, and that mentors act as educators and coaches within that environment.

> I see school-based ITE as being chiefly about professional socialization. I don't go along with people who say that what you do at college is a total waste of time, but what you really need is the chance to try things out in a sort of supportive environment. I don't believe in the 'chuck them in at the deep end' approach. For me, being a mentor is about guidance and about asking questions about why they did it like that, and providing suggestions for how to do it in another way. It makes you think much more carefully about what you're doing, too, you know. You have to start to ask yourself questions and examine your motives behind, I mean your values really behind, what you do.
>
> (Mentor)

More specifically, students can expect to look to mentors for their experience and expertise in:

- thinking open-mindedly about what and how to teach and how to behave as a teacher;
- considering the values implicit in their actions and words;
- ways of organizing and managing classrooms;
- planning and developing curricula;
- matching content and teaching styles to the pupils they teach;
- dealing with difficult pupils;
- practical strategies for making lessons run smoothly;
- ways of coping and managing when things go wrong;
- a range of marking and assessment, recording and reporting techniques;
- planning and managing practical work;
- working collaboratively with colleagues;
- relating theory and findings from research to practice;
- giving advice about job applications.

From pupil to teacher

Essentially, mentoring is about helping students to make the transition from being school pupils to being school teachers. Students come to their ITE course with all sorts of experiences, expectations and understandings of schools and schooling, teachers and teaching. These experiences, expectations and understandings, which predominantly originate from thousands of hours spent observing teachers as pupils, from their dealings with them as parents if they are mature students, and from cultural knowledge about what teachers do and what they are like (see Weber and Mitchell 1995), influence their implicit theories of teaching and learning and, therefore, their ideas about the sort of teachers they want to be and be seen as being. In short, student teachers themselves play a central role in their own professional socialization and professional development. It is important for teacher educators, be they HEI lecturers or schoolteacher mentors, actively to recognize and intervene in this process and to hijack what might be described as the student's tacit knowledge (or 'common sense') for positive and productive purposes. Bullough *et al.* (1991: 189–90) put it in the following words:

> . . . the challenge before us is clear: Beginning teachers need to be helped to come to a reasonably full awareness of the conceptions they hold of themselves as teachers and of the origins of the meanings they hold; they need to recapture their histories . . . many of these meanings are unarticulated and taken for granted; they find expression in the teachers' 'common sense' . . . Becoming aware of them is necessary for them to be remade.

Many ITE courses do include some sort of biographical work aimed at helping students to examine where their ideas about schools and teachers come from and mentors may be able to build on this. Whether or not students have already done any work of this kind, a good starting point is to ask them to compare the schools they attended as pupils with the one in which they are to do their practice. They should focus on such things as:

- school aims;
- pupil intake (in terms of social class, academic ability, sex, racial mix);
- teaching styles;
- subjects taught;
- examination results;
- how discipline is maintained and what sanctions are used;
- organizational features (e.g. Does the school have houses or year groups or both? Are pupils streamed or set or banded? Are pupils appointed as prefects?);
- extracurricular activities.

When this has been done, mentors should guide the students in looking at the underlying values and the circumstantial and contextual features which lead to schools and teachers approaching things in different ways. For instance, students should be alerted to such things as the effect that competition between neighbouring schools can have on organization and declared ethos, to the way in which the social and ethnic composition of the pupil population and pupil cultures interact with teachers' and institutional aims and values, and to how having a split site influences what goes on.

In addition, students could also spend some time with individual pupils, collecting information about the youngsters' educational careers, and investigating if and how these differ from their own experiences. This work might be undertaken as an extension of a 'pupil-tracking' exercise. Useful questions that students might ask of these pupils include:

- types of schools attended;
- favourite subjects;
- views of schools;
- thoughts on how they are perceived and assessed by their teachers – that is, do they think that teachers see them as 'good' pupils, and what constitutes 'good' in the eyes of the school?;
- do they think that all pupils at the school have 'equal opportunities'?; if not, which pupils don't, and why?;
- positive and negative experiences in school;
- ideas of what characteristics are possessed by 'good' and 'bad' teachers;
- favourite occupations outside school;
- what do the pupils want to do when they leave school.

Tasks of this nature could be done during the 'induction' or 'orientation' period of the placement. They can be extremely valuable because they help to make the 'taken for granted' problematic and, thereby, encourage questioning and criticality. Asking questions and being critical is an essential part of the student teacher's socialization and professional development, not least because, unless and until they do begin to examine what has happened to them, the majority tend to assume that, basically, their educational experiences are not substantially different from those of other people (see Sikes and Troyna 1991). They have, however, generally had positive and privileged experiences of schools and schooling, which are by no means 'normal'. These experiences can lead to them holding particular conceptions of pupils and of themselves as teachers, which selectively colour how they make sense of the ITE input they receive. For instance, they may find it difficult to imagine, or put themselves into the position of, the pupils who, they are told, are disaffected, are not interested in school work, and are not concerned to conform to school rules and values. Similarly, and at the same time, they may hold on to a notion of themselves as teachers who motivate and inspire all pupils, even the disaffected ones, simply through their enthusiasm and love for their subject. Having such views is likely to affect the significance they give to what they are told in the HEI. Even the reality of school practice may have minimal impact because student teachers often tell themselves that things will be different once they start working as 'real' teachers in schools of their own choice.

Various research projects have found that teachers often finish short (e.g. one-year postgraduate certificate in education) ITE courses little changed from when they entered, in terms of their ideas about teaching, learning and schooling (see Bullough et al. 1991). This is probably because their ideas and expectations are not challenged and because they have little opportunity to try out any alternative visions that they may have. Mentors working in school-based ITE schemes are in an ideal position to help to provide a break in what is so often a process through which new teachers uncritically reproduce their own educational experiences. The key word here is 'uncritical'. It may well be appropriate for a student teacher to teach in the way that he or she was taught, but the task of the mentor is to make the student aware that there are other ways of doing things which may be more appropriate or more effective. In our view, mentoring is fundamentally about (a) helping students to look beyond their own limited experiences and (b) providing strategies to assist them to think like teachers rather than pupils. It is about facilitating the development of a professional persona, and this can clearly be done most effectively through contextualized practical experience in school where there are pupils to try it out on.

Despite, and perhaps because of, their extensive experience in schools as pupils, student teachers have to be shown, and have to learn, how to do what teachers do. They have to learn how to think and how to behave like a teacher. Among other things, they have to learn how to match what they teach and how they teach it to the different pupils they encounter, and they have to learn how to have the most professionally positive and productive relationships with these pupils. Above all, student teachers have to learn that being in school as a teacher is very different to being there as a pupil. This can be a difficult lesson, especially for those who have chosen to teach because they themselves enjoyed school.

Developing a professional persona

Sooner or later most teachers do develop professional personas; they learn how to be teachers. Much of the learning occurs as the result of experience of teaching but some of it is age-related. For instance, 'mature' students, particularly perhaps those with their own children, often experience fewer difficulties than younger ones when it comes to establishing professional relationships with pupils. This is largely because of how pupils perceive and relate to them as older people *per se* and how they perceive and relate to the pupils as 'children' or young people. Although being on a school-based ITE course will not have much impact on what might be described as age-related learning, it should expedite practical and experiential learning simply because it provides more opportunities for such learning to take place. The intention is that they become better, more effective teachers sooner than they would have done through traditional ITE. This will not, however, happen automatically; it has to be planned for.

Planning for the development of the professional persona takes place at various levels and involves different people. We assume that HEI and school-based mentors work closely in planning and organizing students' overall school experience. What we are thinking about in this chapter, though, is the work that goes on within a specific school and which involves specific teachers. As well as having some shared aims and values, it is likely that these specific teachers each hold their own views and philosophies regarding teaching and being a teacher, learning and schooling. We would suggest that at an early stage in the planning of school-based work, it is important for all teachers involved as mentors to explore and explicate these in much the same way as the students are required to (we make further suggestions as to how this might be done in Chapter 7). Such an exercise will not necessarily be easy because, with time and experience, a lot of what teachers do as teachers becomes second-nature. What they have learnt through practical experience becomes part of their tacit and taken-for-granted knowledge and as such is not easy to get hold of. However, there are considerable benefits to be gained from adopting just such a critical and reflective approach and teachers who have done so as part of their mentoring work have expressed the view that being theoretical about being practical has been both professionally and personally rewarding (see HMI 1995: 2, 5).

> Teachers always say that they haven't got the time to stop and think about what they're doing and I used to say that just as much as anyone, but I don't really think it's true, it's an excuse. My wife trained as a primary teacher and they did an awful lot about this idea of the reflective practitioner, but I can't remember anything about that in my secondary training. Most of what we did was to do with teaching the subject. I don't think I ever really systematically thought about what I did in the classroom or as a teacher more generally till I became a mentor and got involved in that. And I don't think I'd have been able to tell you. But on reflection it's obvious, you are better able to do anything if you understand why you do it rather than just how to do it. I mean, we've moved away from that approach in Maths, from the sort of, all you need to know is how to do it, not why it works, the thinking is that you need to know both, so it stands to reason it applies to most things really. Anyway, I've now thought a lot more about my philosophy and values if you like, as a teacher, as well as about things like establishing control, so that I can be a better mentor and I think the benefits have been more to me than to the student teachers really.
>
> (Subject mentor)

Requiring mentors to reflect on their own practice means taking an approach which demands a lot of work from them. We make no apology for this because, as we have made clear, on our view, mentoring primarily places the emphasis on teachers' thinking, on what Elbaz (1983) terms 'practical professional knowledge'. As well as requiring mentors rigorously to interrogate their own professional values and practices, such an emphasis and approach means consciously and systematically thinking about what individual student teachers need to know, and what experiences they should have in order to enable them to become effective and reflective teachers. How can they best be helped?

Knowing the students: Matching programmes to needs

To a considerable extent, effective mentoring means taking an individualized approach. Students arrive on ITE courses and in schools having had a range of different experiences. There will be those who have already done a great deal of teaching work in one form or another; for instance, they may have been responsible for training new workers in a previous career, or they may have brought up their own children. Some may have worked as Sunday School teachers, on summer schemes and camps, or sports or music coaching courses. Others, however, will themselves be straight from school or university. One size of ITE programme does not fit everyone and some degree of 'tailoring' is essential if all student teachers are to achieve their full potential. The principle of matching applies just as much here as it does when teaching pupils, and mentors will probably decide that explicitly involving student teachers in planning their individual programmes can be valuably used as a modelling exercise in how to plan pupil learning. (The case study at the end of this chapter, which was written jointly by a schoolteacher mentor and an HEI tutor, highlights some of the issues surrounding catering for individual needs.)

In Chapter 4, we mentioned possible sources of information about students. These include curricula vitae and reports from the HEI and other schools in which students may have been placed. In addition, it is useful, at the outset, to make time for individual interviews in which mentors can get to know something about students and discover what they see their own needs as being. As well as communicating verbally, students can be asked to write down their aims and concerns for the practice. They may, for instance, be apprehensive about their ability to establish classroom control, or may want to focus on their questioning technique. Requiring that time is spent on looking at their professional needs and articulating them is especially valuable because it puts an emphasis on reflection and demonstrates to the student that school-based programmes are not just about 'doing' but rather are concerned with thinking about doing. It also gets students to take some responsibility for their own professional development. While a national Career Entry Profile is likely to become a statutory requirement, the majority of ITE schemes presently use some sort of record of personal achievement or development, which, in itself, requires students to engage in this type of reflection. This could be a useful starting point. Alternatively, or in addition, mentors might like to consider getting students to keep journals in which they record and analyse selected aspects and areas of their professional experience (see Holly 1989). Not only are these of immediate use but they can prove to be a valuable tool for personal and professional development throughout a teacher's career. (In fact, we recommend that mentors should themselves keep journals and we look at the topic in more detail in Chapter 7.)

Having got information about individual students' needs, mentors are then in a stronger position to plan a detailed programme which is likely to consist of focused observations, collaborative and independent teaching, feedback, information and seminar type sessions, and space for students to pursue their own professional interests should they wish to do so. In the rest of this chapter, the focus is on observation, collaborative and independent teaching, encouraging good equal opportunities practice and how to deal with students who are having problems. Issues associated with assessment are dealt with in a separate chapter.

Observation: Students observing teachers

Observation has been and continues to be a central feature of most forms of ITE. Whether it is students observing experienced teachers or teachers observing students, there has to be a clear understanding of the purposes of observation and of what the various participants are bringing to it. Planning and preparation are essential if the full benefits of the exercise are to be obtained.

When students first observe teachers teaching, it is likely that their perspective will have more in common with that of a pupil than that of a teacher. What they 'see' will be coloured both by their own experiences as pupils in classrooms, and by their ideas about the sort of teacher they want to be and be seen as being. For instance, if they want to be a teacher who passes on knowledge to enthusiastic, motivated and quiet pupils, they may be shocked when they observe someone committed to experiential and participatory learning in operation. They may even judge a teacher who works in such a way to be a 'bad' teacher, because they are applying a particular set of criteria which do not match the teacher's own and which may be inappropriate in that particular context. Students need, therefore, to be helped to observe classrooms from the point of view of the teachers teaching in them. They also need to be absolutely clear as to the purpose of any observation and of the contribution it can make to their professional development. This could be helpfully set down in a document lodged in the school's ITE reference file and a copy could also be given to each student. An example follows:

Observation

Effective observation of colleagues at work can and should play a crucial role in the professional development of all teachers, regardless of how experienced they are. We learn how to do many things by observation and teaching is no exception. As a student teacher, you will be spending quite a bit of time on observations and, if you are to gain the maximum benefit, it is important for you to be clear on a number of points. These are as follows:

- You are observing in order to learn how to teach. While you may not always agree with what you see, you are not there to criticize in a negative manner.
- What you observe should be confidential between you, the teacher and the pupils. In exceptional cases, it may be your professional duty to report what you see. In such cases, consult either your professional or subject mentor.
- Open, unfocused observations are of limited value. You need to focus your observations on one or two carefully defined areas. These areas may be related to your own learning targets or to an aspect of their practice that the teacher wishes to have feedback on. Do negotiate the agenda before conducting the observation.
- Find out as much background information as you can: Where does the lesson fit in terms of what has gone before and what is to come? What are the teacher's aims and objectives? How do pupils usually respond? Has anything happened which is likely to affect their response?
- Agree on how the observation will be conducted. Decide, in consultation with the teacher, such matters as where you are to sit and whether you should help pupils.
- Decide how you are to record your observations and ensure that you have all the necessary equipment to hand.
- Fix a time for feedback and debriefing.
- Phrase any comments or questions in a constructive way. If you do not agree with how something has been done, ask 'Why did you. . .?'
- Thank the teacher for sharing their lesson with you.
- Following the observation and the feedback, write a summary of what you have learnt.

Observation is not just, or even not primarily, about watching what teachers do with a view to emulating their practice. Indeed, as was discussed in relation to the apprenticeship model of ITE, it is arguable whether 'copying' teachers' practice is possible. As Tomlinson (1995: 14) notes:

> . . . the demands of teaching are *complex*, it involves a lot going on at once and much of this is relatively unpredictable or *open*, yet requiring immediate coping. Like many such capabilities, these features make teaching 'messy', which is one reason why it's difficult for the novice to see *how* the effective teacher is actually doing it. They're probably doing it differently from any other teachers; complex activities like teaching and learning typically allow many ways. However they're doing it, they're almost certainly doing a lot of things at once, and typically they'll be doing them in a fluent and more or less intuitive way which they may find difficult to consciously describe.

It is difficult, if not impossible, for an outsider to understand everything that is going on in a particular classroom because they are unlikely to know all the antecedent details. In their book on classroom observation, Rob Walker and Clem Adelman (1975) told the story of how they were completely non-plussed when the pupils in a class they were observing for research purposes kept calling out 'Strawberries! Strawberries!'. It was only later that they learnt that this referred back to a previous lesson when the teacher had likened certain experiences to strawberries – pleasant enough at the time but not very substantial. Consequently, when the teacher talked about similar experiences, the pupils had recalled the strawberries example as a sort of private joke. Similarly, observers will not know the relationships between pupils and between teacher and pupils, or about common experiences which influence and shape the way in which particular lessons develop. Because of relational factors and because so much depends upon the personal characteristics of each teacher, teaching cannot be simplistically reproduced and replicated. Students can, however, learn what might be described as 'generic' professional skills or strategies, for example techniques of behaviour management, classroom organization and questionning. They can see how a particular teacher responds to a particular incident, or how they organize their teaching in a particular context and, provided that they are aware of the situational nature of the things that teachers do, they can store that information away in their professional knowledge bank to be brought out, adapted and applied in future appropriate circumstances.

If they are to get any value from their observations, students therefore need to be given a minimum of background information. At the least they need to know:

- the teacher's aims and objectives for the lesson;
- the teacher's 'philosophy' concerning teaching and learning;
- where the lesson fits in terms of what has gone before and what is to come;
- something about relationships within the class;
- the nature and range of pupil aptitude and ability;
- constraining factors, such as the size and layout of the available teaching space.

Observations should be focused on some particular aspect of teaching practice, such as questioning technique, beginning and ending lessons, use of resources, teacher–pupil interactions, or pupil responses and behaviours. Indeed, teachers may choose to 'kill two birds with one stone' by asking students to give them feedback on an area of their practice about which they are concerned, or which they feel that they are not in a position adequately to monitor themselves. Similarly, students may decide to link their observation to their own personal targets or to the competences specified in assessment profiles. 'Open' observations, where students just go in and comment generally, are of limited value because so many things are going on that it is difficult for even experienced observers, let alone a 'novice', to 'see' anything with any degree of clarity or acuity.

> I like to take advantage of having students in to observe to do some research into my own teaching. I think that you can meet your own needs while you're meeting theirs. The usual thing is to get them to look at how you talk to kids, who you talk to, things like that and you can get some really interesting information back from a straightforward tally count sort of thing, you know, where they just record who you speak to and what sort of interaction it is. Because you don't always see it for yourself. Like, for instance, a few years ago I asked someone to do that and the outcome was that I had far, far more to do with the boys in the class than with the girls. But if you'd asked me I'd have said I was pretty even-handed. And when you have that sort of evidence it makes you stop and think and try to do something about it. Recently, I got a student to look at the sort of questions I ask and so the outcome was that I've been working on asking more open questions, rather than closed and rhetorical ones all the time.
>
> (Subject mentor)

What is important is that, over the period of time available for this work, students should have the opportunity to observe a range of different teaching situations, a range of styles and approaches, and that their observations should include a variety of different foci. Subject and professional mentors in negotiation with students should devise a programme of observation for the students. As well as observing in their own subject, it will be useful for them to observe in other areas too, not least because they may come to these with fewer assumptions and may, therefore, be able to see what is going on with a more open mind.

There are, of course, various ways of actually recording observations. Which approach is chosen will depend upon the particular nature and focus of the observation itself. On occasion, an observation schedule with pre-specified types of behaviour to be recorded may be appropriate (e.g. features of behaviour management); in other cases, a more discursive account may be better (e.g. giving instructions); sometimes a graphical or mapping approach may be required (e.g. classroom management and organization). It is important to stress that it is observed behaviour that should be recorded, rather than the student's interpretations of that behaviour. Learning to note what has happened rather than what you think has happened is not easy, but is essential if students are to move beyond the taken-for-granted assumptions and preconceptions based on their own experiences and values.

Having undertaken and completed observations, students need to be helped and guided in their analysis of what was going on. Without some discussion between the observer and the observed, much of the value of the exercise is lost. The teacher being observed may, for instance, want to explain why they did something in a certain way, or the student may wish to seek clarification on a particular point. It is only through discussions of this nature that students can gain access to teacher thinking, which is the aim of the observation. Time for this must, therefore, be built into the programme.

Teachers observing students

(Formal observation of students for assessment purposes will be dealt with in Chapter 6.) As has been noted, within ITE the main purpose of observation is to provide an opportunity for teachers and students to reflect on what happens during lessons (or other encounters between teachers and pupils, such as form periods or in extracurricular activities) with a view to refining future practice on the basis of analysis of what is observed. There is absolutely no point to observation without critical analysis. Everyone, however experienced they are, can learn from watching other people teach, and it is important that those who take on the responsibility of being mentors – or observers – are comfortable with this notion. Taking a superior attitude, or failing to take the opportunity to gain new insights into teaching practice and teacher thinking, are indications of an impoverished professional attitude.

I had an embarrassing incident last year when I had to tell someone that I didn't want them to be a mentor any more. Oh, it was awful.

It was bad for me on a personal level, having to tell him, but it was also very worrying because that person continues to teach in the school . . . I'd had my reservations about him anyway but there didn't seem to be anyone else who could take on mentoring in that department, all the other people were fairly new appointments and the head of department had another major responsibility. On reflection it would've been better to let one of the newer people do it . . . The students concerned eventually came to me and said that they didn't think that their mentor was very helpful and that everything they said or did was criticized out of hand, but there weren't any concrete suggestions made for how to improve. The only thing that was acceptable was to do it exactly like the mentor did it – and then it wasn't good enough either. Now that's not to my mind the way to do it. And of course the students had compared notes with their friends and they'd realized that they were getting a poor deal and I had to agree. When I spoke to the person concerned I was shocked that he couldn't see there was anything in it. His view was that the students were the absolute beginners who sort of had to sit at his feet. The result was that I now have a very negative view of him because I can see this pig-headed, supercilious attitude coming across in other areas too. I just don't think he is a very good teacher anymore.

(Professional mentor)

If it is to be an effective strategy for teaching and learning, observation of students has to be regular, positive and constructive in character, focused, contextualized, followed by timetabled feedback sessions, confidential and matched to the needs of the individual. Each programme has its own requirements in terms of the number of times that students should be formally observed, but apart from this mentors have to know their students and gauge what is likely to be most useful for them. The student's confidence, whether it is their first or second time in school, the time they have had to establish relationships with classes, the type of teaching they are doing, and so on, all have to be taken into account. One constant, however, is that students should always know when observers are intending to come in. Some people believe that an element of surprise is desirable because it makes it impossible for students to prepare 'special performances', but this doesn't allow for the development of a consensual, negotiated, partnership approach to learning to teach and, therefore, has no part to play in any mentoring programme.

It is crucial when planning a student's timetable, and hence the times when they can be observed, that the timetables of the people who will be observing them are also taken into account. Feedback and debriefing should happen as close to the event as possible or much of their value is lost. This is a difficult area but one which schools do have to try to come to grips with if their ITE work is to be effective.

> It is a problem and it's one that we are well aware of. I don't think that we had initially realized the implications because the first year in the scheme you'd observe a student on a Monday morning and you probably wouldn't get a chance to sit down with them properly until say Thursday afternoon. You know what I mean. We've tried to do better since then because if you leave it so long you both forget, the student teaches other classes and you lose it somehow.
>
> (Subject mentor)

> To be honest I've not found the feedback as much use as it could be because there's never time straight after the lesson. They've always got to run off to their next class. What would be best would be if they could sit down with you straight after, or within the half day, and go through it, because by the time they do get round to it so much else has happened.
>
> (Student)

In 'the olden days' it was not unusual for supervisors from the HEI or members of the school staff to appear in a classroom, sit and observe all or part of a lesson, write a critique and then disappear. Those of us who were subjected to this ordeal often experienced observation as threatening, if not confrontational; it made very little contribution to our professional development. The mentoring approach, however, places the emphasis on negotiation and consensual planning. Thus students should have some input into decisions about what the focus of observations should be. This does not mean that they should always specify the focus, but rather that student and observer should have some shared overview of (a) the student's progress to date and (b) what they need to work on presently and in the future. Taking this approach means mapping out, setting and working towards specific targets. Observation and feedback are the mechanisms for achieving this.

An important implication of observation according to this model is that the observer keeps to the agreed agenda. If they have said that they will focus on, for example, questioning technique, then feedback should deal only with this. Other areas of practice, or issues arising, should be kept for future observations. Of course, it is not always this straightforward. Plans can be overtaken by events and lessons can take totally unexpected directions, which may have to be dealt with immediately, but the general rule should be that the pre-specified focus should be maintained.

Observers should limit their observations to what they see and hear. As was mentioned earlier, it can be extremely difficult not to make interpretational and evaluatory comments, and it is probably even harder for experienced teachers to resist the temptation to do so than it is for students! However innocent or well-meant they are, such comments are not necessarily as helpful to the student's own professional development as are questions, based on the evidence, which encourage them to explore the reasons why they think they did things, or why events unfolded in the way that they did. It follows from this that it is the student, rather than the mentor, who should be doing most of the talking during the feedback sessions. To reiterate, the point of feedback and debriefing is to provide a basis for future development. Students must be able to make use of what is said, so the whole tenor of the session should be positive and constructive. Almost inevitably there will be times when mentors feel that students have done silly things, created difficult situations for themselves, or even worse, but it has to be continually borne in mind that the mentor has accrued professional and contextual knowledge that the student does not have access to. Indeed, it is one of the functions of the feedback sessions to provide such contextual knowledge (although, as far as possible, students should already have researched for themselves, or been appraised of, significant information of this kind). Getting cross with the student or making disparaging comments may relieve some of the mentor's anger or frustration but does not create an effective learning situation.

> We had a bit of a do last week with M. and some of the teachers came to me very angry about him. You see we'd given him some IT work because he said he'd taught it at the university, but it turned out that he didn't know the particular software or the PC they were using and he was just keeping one step ahead. He'd already told me that when he'd told the head of department this the response had been that he ought to buy the equipment and familiarize himself with it at home, which I thought was a bit much because I think things are quite tight for him, financially. He's got a wife and children. But anyway, it seems that in the lesson he'd set them some task and he was going round helping them and he'd accidentally lost all this girl's work so he was working with her, trying to retrieve it and the rest of the class just had to get on with it. There's a group of girls in the class who're all right if you keep on at them but M. was working with this girl. He told me he felt really bad about what had happened and that he had an idea that something was going on over in the corner but he thought it was just that they were restless. Jayne was observing him but she'd got involved in helping some other kids because M. didn't know what he was doing really. Anyway, the lesson ended but at break time these notices had gone up all over the school saying So and So is a Slag. And So and So had gone to her head of year in great distress, weeping

and wailing and the head of year came at me because it turned out that the notices had been printed out in M.'s lesson by that group of girls. And he hadn't had a clue, but nor had Jayne. He should have done things very differently – and so perhaps should she. And apparently she gave him a bollocking in the so-called feedback session because the head of year had had a go at her, and so it goes. Not a very positive experience all round.

(Professional mentor)

The above account raises issues to do with the practical conduct of observations. What exactly should observers do when they are in the classroom? To some extent, the answer depends upon the focus of the observation: there are occasions when constant and total attention to the observation is necessary but others when it is not – if the beginning or ending of a lesson is under attention, for instance. Observer and student need to be clear about what the observer's role should be and, wherever possible, they should keep to what has been agreed. This is not always easy, especially when the observer knows that an intervention on their part could dramatically improve the situation for the student. Pupils also need to be told what is expected of them *vis-à-vis* the observing teacher, for instance whether or not they can ask for help. This whole area is one that is very familiar to researchers working in classrooms. In guides to research it is often addressed under the heading of 'researcher reflexivity', with the key question being how, or is it possible, to minimize the effect on 'normality' that having additional people in the classroom inevitably has? A strategy that is frequently suggested is to explain to the pupils exactly what is going on, what all participants will be or are likely to be doing, and what they themselves should do. The argument is that it is impossible to change the dynamics created by having observers present but that honesty and a straightforward approach reduces the novelty of the situation which, therefore, restores some sense of the *status quo*. Having said this, students, pupils and teachers are all well aware of the circumstances they are in and for the greater part this just has to be accepted. To a certain extent also, now that students do spend more time in school being observed by teachers, it does become a more 'normal' experience. Some teachers have remarked that some pupils are more inclined to treat students they have got to know over an extended period as 'proper' teachers, and that the attitude described in the following quotes is less prevalent than it used to be:

I remember having students when I was at school and they were fair game. You'd play them up, see what you could get away with, it's human nature really and I think you have to expect it because that's what it's about.

(Student)

We all have those stories don't we, about kids being difficult when you're a student. I remember when I was on school practice and I had this class, they were buggers most of the time but just in a mischievous way, not maliciously, and when my supervisor came in they were butter wouldn't melt. And I was grateful but it was a sort of a game. I think it's different though when it's the school and their normal teachers who're doing the supervising. It depends on relationships because I'm afraid I have been aware of teachers who'd play up to their class with the intention of making the student appear to be less competent than they actually were.

(Mentor)

Just as it is useful for students to observe a range of different teachers, so it can be useful for a number of people, in addition to the student's mentors, to provide feedback. Everyone has a different perspective and, even though a specific focus has been agreed, different people will see and pick up on different things and will, subsequently, ask different questions, thus helping students to take a wider view of their practice. These differences in perception can be capitalized upon and joint observations of students who are considered to be having problems can be a useful safeguard against partisan judgements. In every case, however, it is important that all observers should keep to the same conventions and that they should provide written feedback, copied to the mentor.

Collaborative teaching

Focused and guided observation of experienced teachers offers students the opportunity to develop their professional perception by analysing and thinking theoretically about what happens in specific classroom situations. Collaborative teaching takes this process further by allowing them to work alongside experienced teachers and share in, variously, the planning, preparation, teaching and evaluation of lessons. Traditionally, collaborative teaching has not been that common in ITE – or in schools generally for that matter. Teachers have tended to work alone and in privacy. This has meant that professional thinking and practice have not been shared as effectively as they might have been, to the detriment of teachers and pupils alike.

Collaborative teaching in an ITE context refers to lessons jointly planned and taught by students and experienced teachers. Various degrees of collaboration can be involved, from the teacher simply sharing their planning, rationale and long-term thinking for a lesson, which the student then observes and analyses with the teacher, through to equal partnership and participation and on to the student taking the main responsibility. The important thing is that the student has a designated and clearly defined responsibility for and within the lesson which is targeted to advance their learning and their practice. Peter Tomlinson (1995: 51) describes 'progressively collaborative teaching' as involving the student engaging:

> . . . in teaching with another, usually a more experienced teacher-mentor, initially staying very much within the mentor's framework and undertaking limited aspects of teaching with support but progressively trying out and taking on a wider range of more extensive aspects. The progressive nature of this arrangement is important to emphasize; the novice status of student-teachers means not only that they're not in a position to make a full contribution from the outset, but that they need various forms of assistance that are geared to their progress.

The chief benefits of such an approach are that it can give students considerable access to 'real' teacher thinking and that it 'eases them in' in a controlled manner. It can also further the experienced teacher's professional development by explicitly requiring them to reflect on their teaching and by forcing them to articulate their tacit knowledge (see Chapter 7). School-based ITE probably offers greater opportunity for collaborative teaching than 'traditional' ITE does. It does, however, have to be very carefully planned if it is to be truly collaborative and if it is to meet students' needs in a progressive manner. It is also important that students should have the opportunity to work in this way with more than one teacher if they are to have experience of alternative styles, approaches and philosophies. Arranging this can be difficult where colleagues are defensive and reluctant to become involved. However, at the risk of being contentious, perhaps schools where a significant proportion of colleagues do have this attitude are not the best sites for school-based ITE anyway!

No matter how valuable collaborative teaching might prove to be, students do have to have the chance to work independently and to develop their own professional knowledge, their own ideas, strategies, contextual judgements, and their own personal, professional philosophies. Creating a supportive climate in which this can best occur will take a considerable part of the mentor's time.

Individual teaching

> When learning to teach students feel stimulated, apprehensive, exposed, endangered, confused, discouraged, touched, proud and lost – not necessarily in that order.
>
> (Fuller and Brown 1975, quoted in Furlong and Maynard 1995: 68)

The process of acquiring a professional persona as a teacher can be threat-ening and damaging to an individual's sense of self. Mentors need to be aware of this and of the need to incorporate that knowledge into their planning for their students. The issue is, perhaps, most significant when it comes to students working individually as teachers with their 'own' classes. Although she is writing about experienced primary school teachers, what Nias (1989: 25–6) has to say is equally applicable to those working in the secondary sector:

> . . . the historical, financial and philosophical traditions of primary teaching, the culture and physical context of schools, all create a situ-ation in which who and what people perceive themselves to be are seen by those inside and outside the profession to matter as much as what they can do. As a result, teachers expect the job to make exten-sive calls upon the personality, experience, preferences, talents, skills, ideas, attitudes, values and beliefs of each individual. Equally, they expect the freedom to ensure that the ways in which, and still to some extent what, they teach are consistent with the values which are most salient to them. Primary teaching as an occupation makes heavy demands upon the self.

Student teachers can find that they experience tension and conflict between their notions concerning the sort of teacher they want to be and the sort of teacher that they feel circumstances of various kinds 'force' them to be, and also the sort of teacher other people (colleagues, pupils, parents, etc.) see them as being and expect them to be. Because teaching is, in many respects, a very personal and very personally demanding type of occupation, such tensions and conflicts can cause the individual grave distress and can lead to them questioning their involvement in, and com-mitment to, the profession.

Although the attitudes of other members of staff can contribute to students' difficulties in this area, it is suggested that this threat to their sense of self most often crystallizes around the business of discipline and control. Being able to maintain discipline and control in a way that meets their own personal standards (and it is a very personal thing as all teachers know) is the issue which seems most to exercise and concern students and newly qualified teachers. Tomlinson (1995: 119–20) suggests that inexpe-rienced (and unsuccessful) students and teachers have a 'tendency to sep-arate management of pupil behaviour from promoting learning, as tends to be implied by such sayings as "first you've got to achieve discipline and order, then you can teach them" '. In reality, it is not as simple as this, not least because if schools are to achieve their aim of teaching effectively, they rely upon a consensual relationship between teachers and pupils in which pupils behave and learn and teachers 'manage' and teach. What student teachers have to learn is how to establish a professional persona and professional relationships which expedite this process and which also allows them to maintain a self-image that they are happy with.

> I think one of the most difficult things that sometimes has to be got over is when students want to be friends with the kids and this can cause them all sorts of problems. I think most of them go through it and that's where this 'don't smile until Christmas' thing comes in. You know, go in hard and then you can loosen up does tend to be better for most people. I had this lecturer at college and I'll always remember her saying 'you need to get rid of this idea that you're going to be friends. They don't want to be your friend. They've got their own mates and they don't need or want you and it'd be a bit peculiar if they did. You're a teacher to teach them, not to be their chum'. I thought at the time that she had the wrong attitude because I was going to go in and be like the big brother and they were going to learn for me because they loved me and all that. Experience teaches though.
>
> (Subject mentor)

> We've been told all this about not being too friendly because if you are the kids will take advantage of you and I'm unsure because I do want to be friends and have good relationships because I think they are essential.
>
> (Student)

Mentors can help in so far as they can decide which classes students will teach. Knowing the particular pupils concerned, they can also contextualize the 'tips' and strategies that they pass on. If mentors can help to ensure that students do achieve some measure of success in their dealings with pupils, then they will be doing all that they can to boost their confidence. Feeling confident that they can do it right at least some of the time is crucial if students are to begin to see themselves as competent teachers. Mentors in school-based ITE programmes are in an excellent position to work towards this whereas HEI staff who lack the necessary contextual knowledge cannot provide such useful support.

Equal opportunities practice in school-based ITE

The National Curriculum is an 'entitlement' curriculum; consequently, effective equal opportunities practice is a prerequisite of effective educational practice *per se*. Inspections by the Office for Standards in Education give attention to, and report on, equal opportunities practice, even if the Council for the Accreditation of Teacher Education (CATE) competences do not explicitly refer to it. Some ITE programmes do assess students' equal opportunities practice, although these are probably in the minority. In all cases, though, it is crucial that students are made aware of the issues and of their relevance to classroom practice and to conduct within the school, not least because all teachers now have a legal, as well as a moral, responsibility to ensure that their pupils are not discriminated against nor disadvantaged in any way on such grounds as sex, 'race', physical or mental ability, social class or sexuality. Everyone working in schools also has the basic human right of being treated with respect and sometimes, unfortunately, this has to be spelt out.

> We sometimes have difficulties to do with how they [students] treat the lab technicians. And this isn't unusual; I've talked to people in other schools and they say they have to deal with it too. We have excellent technicians and it makes me really angry to see the way some students behave. They take the attitude that they are superior and they make unreasonable demands and talk in a downright disrespectful way. I do have to say that it's usually the males that do it rather than the women, and sometimes it's the matures that are worst of all. I come down very hard on that sort of thing.
>
> (Science mentor)

Generally, students will attend sessions in the HEI-based component of their course which deal with gender, 'race' and special needs, although this will be variable, both in terms of quality and quantity (cf. Siraj-Blatchford 1993). It is important for mentors to find out what has been done in this area. It is also important to get some idea of each individual's thinking, experience and expertise as it relates to equal opportunities, because this will give clues as to what their needs in this area are. The same goes for teachers who are to be working with students. Despite – some would say because of (e.g. Skeggs 1994) – the legislation there is still a strong feeling current in schools that attention to equal opportunities is 'left-wing' and 'loony'. Some teachers continue to see equal opportunities primarily as a theoretical issue rather than as a fundamental and integral part of their practice.

> I was quite shocked at the attitudes of some of the teachers. I was a personnel manager for a large company before I came on this course so I'm *au fait* with equal opportunities legislation and with the various initiatives in the workplace. I'd assumed that in education things would be that much better than in business, but what I've seen so far suggests that it's the opposite and I've been quite surprised by that.
>
> (Student)

Right from the start of their time in a school, students need to be acquainted with that institution's declared attitude towards equal opportunities, of any policies that there may be, and of procedures to be followed in the event of pupils making racist or sexist remarks. This information should be included in the ITE reference file. Students have to be given examples of, and told what constitutes, unacceptable behaviour, both by pupils and by themselves, because some of them may just not have a clue.

> I got into a bit of trouble at my last school because I said something about Christian names. And I just said it, as you do. The teacher tore in to me and said I should have said first name because most of the kids in the class didn't have Christian names. I didn't know what she was on about until she told me that they were Muslim and Hindu and that to talk about their Christian name was actually offensive to some of them. It had never occurred to me. A friend of mine had a similar experience in a primary school because she was doing some work on farms and pigs and she brought in pork cocktail sausages as a treat!
>
> (Student)

> I was told that my behaviour was sexist and 'out of touch with the real world' because I called the girls dear and asked them to collect in the books and praised them for being quiet and let them always go first. I ask you! It's not me who's out of touch. It's how things are! We had this session in the university on assessment and the lecturer was saying that assessments aren't objective, that different types of test favour different groups and that 11 plus wasn't fair and that more girls than boys should have got places because they did better but they didn't because there were so many places set aside for each sex and sometimes more places were available for lads. Well so what! That's how the world is. I don't need to waste my time on things like that.
>
> (Student)

Student teachers should also be informed about the 'special needs' of any of the pupils that they teach. Without such knowledge, they clearly cannot plan for or properly accommodate such children.

> They hadn't bothered to tell me about the deaf, sorry, hearing-impaired children, at the school. They have quite of few of these in a unit that's attached and these kids spend some of their time in the unit but most of it in the main school. They don't come in for all the classes and they have a teacher for the deaf who comes in to lessons with them. I was really disconcerted by this because I didn't know! For a start there was this other teacher in the classroom and I initially felt a bit threatened by that because she was signing, supposedly what I was saying, but I couldn't really know. And then if I'd known I could have planned work for the kids for the times when they didn't come; I did do this, but not at the start because I just didn't know. The professional mentor told me that it was an oversight, that they'd for-gotten to tell me, but I think it was a big oversight.
>
> (Student)

When it comes to their classroom practice, as a minimum students need guidance and should receive feedback on the following:

- *Planning*: the promotion and realization of equality of opportunity should be integral to their planning. Students should take care to provide experiences, resources and content which do not reinforce and which, wherever possible, positively counteract stereotypical thinking. Any assumptions that students may themselves hold about particular groups of students should be challenged and discussed.
- *Grouping*: students need to be aware of the effects that different ways of grouping pupils can have. For instance, there may be occasions when single-sex groups are likely to result in girls achieving more than they would in mixed groups: friendship groups may mean that pupils self-segregate on grounds of 'race' or language. What are the implications of this? Students must make their grouping/organizational decisions with such issues in mind.
- *Use of resources*: resources of all kinds (e.g. books, equipment, teacher or other adult assistance) should be properly accessible to all according to their needs. Resources should present positive, rather than stereotypical, images.
- *Interactions/relationships*: students should be encouraged to monitor the way in which they relate and respond to the pupils in their classes. They should take care to give each pupil the attention they need and are entitled to.
- *Language*: students must think about their use of language. Calling female colleagues or pupils 'love' may cause offence, as may asking Muslim pupils for their Christian name. In the attempt to develop positive relationships or to motivate pupils, teachers sometimes appeal to stereotypical role models or assumptions without considering that these can offend or exclude pupils. Comments like 'the girls will know about the cleansing properties of detergent' are best avoided.

Unfortunately, sexism and racism, sexual and racial harassment do occur in schools and in HEIs, and research (e.g. Menter 1989; Siraj-Blatchford 1993) indicates that it is a not uncommon feature of ITE. It is possible that school-based ITE makes students even more vulnerable to, and at greater risk of, sexist and racist behaviour. For instance, if the perpetrator is a mentor, students may be reluctant to complain for fear of jeopardizing their assessment. The student referred to in the following account could well have been at risk:

> I phoned the professional mentor up and said I was concerned about Luke. The school had said he was failing and would a science tutor go and observe him. So Bert went and he said Luke was OK and that the head of department had agreed. Anyway, I said this to the professional

mentor and she said, 'Really? Well the university's standards must have fallen then'. And I said, as diplomatically as I could, that I was concerned that Luke might be being judged negatively because he's unconventional – he wears an earring and they fancy themselves at that school because they compete with quite a few independents you see. 'Oh no', said the mentor, 'there's no fear of that. The head of his department is a Sikh, so she's well used to unusual people'.

(University tutor)

There needs to be someone within the school who students feel they can confide in if need be. Early on in the programme it is useful for the professional mentor to raise this issue explicitly. It is also helpful if the professional mentor can rely on other teachers in the school having an appropriate attitude towards this area and we will touch on this in Chapter 7.

Students who have problems

Fortunately, only a minority of students have problems that are so severe that they are in danger of 'failing'. Problems should be picked up and addressed as early as possible and students should be made aware of, and helped to remedy, what is going wrong. No-one should come to the end of their course and find out, to their surprise, that they are likely to fail. Each scheme will have its own guidelines, procedures and deadlines for dealing with serious difficulties and mentors should thoroughly familiarize themselves with these. Not keeping to such procedures can lead to difficulties with students formally contesting 'failure' assessments.

I had this situation with a maths student who I was the professional tutor for. I'd gone into school for my one routine visit and the professional mentor said she wanted to have a word with me about Sean. She said 'We're very concerned about Sean. He isn't doing very well at all'. This was two weeks before the end of the practice. So I said, 'Oh, why haven't you phoned me?', and she didn't really answer. She said, 'The Maths Department would like to speak to you'. Well, the head of department was out so I saw someone else and the long and the short of it was that they didn't think his professional knowledge was up to it, they thought his planning and preparation weren't very good, they didn't think he listened to advice, especially if it was given by women, they didn't think he had much time or respect for women anyway. There was also some resentment about him not turning up on a bowling trip that he said he'd go to. They questioned his commitment to teaching, so basically they didn't think he should pass. I asked them if they'd talked to him and they assured me that they had. I have to say that I was astounded because he'd always struck me as an extremely committed student. So I got him in the room and I said, 'How're you doing?', and he said 'Fine. I did have a few problems but they're all sorted out now'. So I thought 'Oh no!'. So I told him what they'd said and I thought he was going to cry, in fact he did. He kept saying 'Why didn't they say these things to me?', and I said they said they had. He said that he'd changed his way of planning four times to do what they'd asked him and each time it wasn't any good. He said that his car had broken down when he should have been at the bowling trip and that he'd phoned the Bowl up to let them know. It was awful. When I got back to the university I phoned the maths tutor and asked if he was aware of all this and he wasn't, but he said he'd go in and sort things out. I couldn't do anything about the subject complaints you see, but I did say that they should have got in touch with me far sooner. It was awful.

(University professional tutor)

Certain steps can be taken to ensure that the possibility of failure is anticipated and, to an extent, avoided:

- get to know students as well as possible – how they approach challenges, how they react to constructive criticism, for example;
- take into account the student's background and experience;
- have regular formal meetings with groups of students and encourage them to share what will certainly be common problems rather than feel obliged to keep them hidden;
- make it easy for individuals to talk to mentors without feeling that it is an unforgivable admission of failure or a last step;
- make it easy for the students to have informal contact with mentors and other members of staff;
- encourage an open atmosphere in which experienced teachers as well as students can share their problems;
- use active listening skills;
- try to deal with problems early and at a low level before they get too serious;
- be sure to follow all early warning and notification procedures to the letter.

Sometimes, difficulties are experienced by the student due to personal or family circumstances. If they confide in someone about such problems, then the mentoring team should be informed of the need to be especially supportive. The HEI should also be told.

Crises do arise, of course, in spite of all efforts to anticipate them. They may well be concerned with relationships, clashes of personality or failure in the classroom. Try to:

- separate real issues from apparent symptoms;
- separate issues from emotions;
- be analytical;
- take it seriously;
- try to offer a range of real strategies to deal with problems, not just palliatives; for example, provide extra practice in appropriate areas; offer guided observation by the student of teachers demonstrating specific competences with follow-up tutorial work; additional observation of the student with post-observation tutorials; visits by HEI tutors;
- honestly ask if it is entirely the student's failure or if any members of staff bear any responsibility;
- give the student a fair chance – don't be hasty or prejudiced, and resist the temptation to write anybody off;
- make sure that it is professional performance rather than personality that is being judged;
- ensure that the student is observed by a number of teachers to get a range of views;
- inform and discuss the situation with the HEI;
- ensure that formal procedures are followed accurately.

There may be occasions when the student does have to be removed from the situation. This stage should, of course, only be reached when all other strategies have been tried. Inevitably people are likely to feel that they have failed, so there must be a thorough debriefing and evaluation.

> We all felt terrible about Casper but there was no way he could stay. He said some unacceptable things to some teachers – one said to me that had it been another teacher she would have gone straight to her union. Frankly he wasn't well, I don't think and we had real cause to be concerned that he might do something to someone. You can't have that.
>
> (Professional mentor)

There is a dilemma in establishing clear and open communication with a student who is in danger of failing, in that building teaching competence is closely connected with the growth of self-confidence. Thus mentors are obliged to tread a difficult line in satisfying the conflicting requirements of clear, prompt communication of concerns and the need to support the student in the nurturing of competence and confidence. Bridges *et al.* (1995: 26) found that:

> If these roles appear to create conflict between their duty to develop and their duty to assess this can impair their ability to carry out these tasks. In the cases studied it was the role of the assessor rather than developer which appeared to suffer.

Jacques (1992: 345) reported similar findings:

> When differences arose the mentors found themselves reluctant to talk about them, convinced that matters would improve. Interestingly, everyone concerned appeared to be collaborators in avoiding the issue. A conspiracy of silence reigned . . .

But even when this is not the case, communications can still go awry for there are those students who, for whatever reason, fail to hear or to understand when they are told that they are having problems:

> We had this student, she was mature, and we were very concerned about her. We told her, we told the university, we had the university tutors in for extra visits but she still didn't seem to grasp what everyone was saying. And it ended up being said in no uncertain terms. After all the helpful and constructive comments, which got us nowhere in terms of her improving, we got more blunt until finally we had this session with her, with me, the subject mentor and the professional and subject tutors from the university and we all put the cards on the table and told her that she was going to fail and that she had to understand that, but I'm not convinced that she did. Her opinion seemed still to be that she was doing OK. What do you do with people like that?
>
> (Professional mentor)

So far, the emphasis has been on student failure, but mentors can fail as well. Mentors also need support and encouragement. Yet with the best will in the world, mentors may come to the point when either they, or someone else, feels that they cannot or should not continue in the role. For this reason, as well as in the event of illness, standby or understudy mentors should be identified at the start of the practice. Although they may not have to undertake any responsibility, this could be a useful form of staff development. It also increases the pool of potential mentors, which means that in future years it may be possible to rotate responsibilities.

The two case studies which follow deal with students who experienced difficulties in their school placements. Readers might like to consider what they would have done had they encountered these students.

Case study: Individual differences – a student with problems

Ideologically, Alan was highly commendable. He had written before the practice to say that he was very interested in sexuality and gender issues and was very keen to use 'creative role-play'. This raised some eyebrows, and staff were awaiting his arrival with some anticipation.

In fact, Alan was a very pleasant, enthusiastic student. However, he always wore a different, ornate earring every day and this did cause some discussion in the mentoring team. A number of staff spoke to him about it, some of whom gave conflicting advice about the desirability of his wearing an earring. As one of his subject mentors, I suggested to him that it was inevitable that there would be differing reactions, but that as long as he was aware of the fact and adopted a range of strategies to deal with it, this would not be a significant issue in the practice as a whole. Unfortunately, I didn't realize that this model of individuals saying different things to him would lead to problems throughout the practice.

A number of teachers talked to Alan about their classes and about the lessons he prepared and taught for them. He appeared not to have prepared material for his lessons and showed me some material for a scheme of work for a Year 9 class given to him by a teacher whose materials are sometimes sexist in nature. Its basis was a story which is centred entirely around two male characters: the only female characters were a silly mother and her naive daughter. Activities included unfocused discussions of, for example, the role of women in society.

After we had discussed the scheme of work, and the mixed gender Year 9 class which he had yet to meet, he decided that the tasks were not appropriate, but insisted on using the story as a basis for work. However, subsequent discussions with the teacher encouraged Alan to only slightly modify the tasks. This was obviously a problem for us to face: how to ensure that the student discusses matters with a range of colleagues, yet develops activities and a style which are based on his own personality and abilities.

The issue surfaced again after Alan had observed another teacher who used drama to confront controversial issues with his Year 9 class. Fired with enthusiasm, Alan created a scheme of work on issues such as racial and sexual attacks in circumstances similar to our own school's inner-city setting, using drama as the major medium. Much of the work involved the children in activities which did not call for them to reflect on what they had been doing, saying and thinking. When Alan talked to me about it, I questioned the range of experiences and activities which the class would go through and whether Alan would be able to carry off such a challenging sequence of lessons. Alan decided to incorporate more written response into the work.

However, the response to the activities from the pupils, and from me as his subject mentor, was not what he'd hoped for. Alan told me that he had asked another teacher to observe and assess one of the role-play lessons and that her report was glowing. I could understand Alan asking her to do this. But I felt a bit miffed when I saw her report in which superlatives prevailed and criticism was scarce: when I observed the class myself, I realized that she was commenting on the material, not on Alan's teaching. When I observed the classes he taught, I wrote reports with positive criticisms, helpful comments and praise where appropriate. What made it worse was that, on her visit to the school, Alan's tutor told me that he had obviously not had a very good practice, but that he had been helped enormously by one particular teacher (not me!) and her observations and comments on Alan's Year 9 class. I felt like spitting actually.

On another occasion, Alan had a staffroom conversation with a teacher who had a very distinctive style of teaching – she used a great deal of humour based upon her knowledge of individual pupils and of the subject matter with which she was working. Alan immediately tried this in a couple of lessons but, of course, failed to carry it off.

By this stage, Alan had lost a lot of confidence. He had been genuinely surprised that so many children lacked motivation and found activities unexciting; he was disappointed by the limitations of the classroom, the need to time and vary activities and by the need to concern himself with trivia such as appropriate stationery not being brought to lessons by the children. His own enthusiasm with ideas was not matched by the children's; his own enthusiasm for teaching was not matched by an understanding of adolescents' levels of understanding or response. He had tried to imitate strategies which were successful for others without attempting to develop his own style and approach. He retreated into an earnestness which was interpreted as humourlessness and as oddity. Pupils openly mimicked him but this he ignored – if only he had been able to laugh at himself and enjoyed, with them, 'the things that make me me'!

Towards the end of his practice, Alan reacted defensively when his work was discussed, just as he was dismissive of pupils who challenged what he'd asked them to do when what they really needed was help to do it. The practice ended with Alan feeling dejected. I could not help but reflect upon why things had gone wrong and how we, as a mentoring team, could have prevented Alan's experience from being so negative.

Case study: Individual differences – a mature student

PGCE [postgraduate certificate in education] students are urged from all sides to incorporate differentiation into their lesson-planning. Yet we suspect that differentiation is not always a prominent

feature of the training these same students receive during their
PGCE course.

These thoughts were prompted by having to deal with a
Science PGCE student in difficulties on his first practice. As we
worked through the various problems arising from his work, we
realized that certain features were familiar. We had heard most of
it before. Not all of it, of course. No two cases are ever quite the
same – but most. The common features were: science student;
usually male; selective school background; industrial experience;
mid to late 30s or early 40s; probably made redundant from his
previous job.

The problems were largely to do with relationships, but perhaps
that is stating the obvious when education is at the heart of things.
In particular, there were examples of troubled relationships with:

- *Pupils*: inappropriate expectations, etc.
- *Teaching staff*: especially when younger than the student.
- *Non-teaching staff*: both in attitude towards and expectations of
  (e.g. unreasonable demands for photocopying, or lack of notice
  for preparation for practical work).

Talking at length to the student helped me to disentangle some of
the factors causing problems. Some cautious generalizations follow.

The older the student, the more likely it is that their own education was in a school quite different from that in which they do
their teaching practice. Many LEAs [local education authorities] did
not go fully comprehensive until the 1970s. Some, of course, still
have not done so. Thus, students' expectations of their pupils can be
unreasonably or unhelpfully high. Or, if nourished by a diet of
tabloid journalism, they can have very low expectations.

Those whose recent 'knowledge' of teachers is largely derived
from the media, and who think that teaching is a relatively simple
occupation, may not take well to being advised or instructed by
teachers younger than themselves, particularly if the latter show no
interest in the kind of work and level of responsibility tackled by
the 'student' in a previous career.

If coming from a job where giving orders to clerical or support
staff was a daily task, it appears that one might omit some of the
interpersonal tact or courtesy that most experienced teachers automatically use with secretaries, caretakers and lab technicians. It is
part of the ethos of a good school to show civility and consideration
to all those who work there. More cynically, one might say that it is
also in a teacher's own interest to get on well with those who can
make his or her own life easier – or much harder. Apparently,
experience and attitudes elsewhere can be quite different.

Then there are the problems of self-esteem and morale that can understandably bedevil people in the immediate aftermath of redundancy.

In many PGCE courses these days, the 'mature' student cannot be simply seen as an oddity. What, then, should one do to help? How might one differentiate for him or her? Tentative suggestions are as follows:

- examine student records before they arrive;
- acknowledge the previous experience of students. Better still, encourage them to contribute from their experience at appropriate points; for example, on experience of appraisal, or as parents themselves, or on dealing with difficult customers;
- ensure that schools are aware of this previous experience. Encourage them to acknowledge, or better still use, it in some way, for example in a Careers session;
- brief all students carefully and tactfully about dealings with teaching and non-teaching staff. Also, brief them on realistic expectations about resources;
- be careful in asking students to teach about a topic in which they have previously specialized. Fine if they can do it well, but 'experts' are not necessarily the best teachers of the utterly inexpert;
- monitor relationships with other, younger students. These can go either way; the older can sometimes resent the younger's apparent success or vice versa.

6 ASSESSMENT

Introduction

Circular 9/92 (DfE 1992) made schools the full partners of higher education not only in the training but also in the assessment of student teachers. However, it did acknowledge that the balance of responsibilities would vary as different partnerships deemed appropriate. The Council for the Accreditation of Teacher Education (CATE 1992: 6) subsequently suggested that schools would normally have 'a leading responsibility' for 'assessing student competences in subject application and classroom skills'. Most schemes have agreed that schools are the partners logically placed to carry the principal responsibility for assessing students' teaching competence, and thus it is that many teachers who traditionally have had little or no role in the formal assessment of trainee teachers (Allsop 1994) now find themselves assuming a major responsibility in this area. It is hardly surprising that teachers often find this one of the most daunting features of school-based initial teacher education (ITE).

> I feel very inadequate in assessing students, and listening to other teachers we feel we are all in the same situation.
>
> (Mentor, quoted in Bridges *et al.* 1995: 23)

> They [the subject mentors] have also got the responsibility – the main responsibility – for passing or failing students and I don't think that's being recognized.
>
> (Professional mentor)

Assessment is an integral part of teachers' jobs, something they are involved in practically every day of their working lives. Many have experience of teacher appraisal and of working as examiners for examination boards. Almost all will have been involved in negotiating pupils' records of achievement and in marking coursework which contributes to public examinations. The recent history of the National Curriculum has left teachers well-versed in the problems and the possibilities of assessment. So why is it that so many teachers are unnerved by the prospect of assessment in the context of ITE?

Is there a problem?

It is the summative element of the assessment process and the possibility of failing individual students which are the most onerous aspects of teachers' new responsibility. Teachers recognize the uniqueness of their own schools and are justifiably concerned that it may be dangerous to generalize from judgements about a student's competence in one establishment to general proficiency. The mentor in an independent school with small classes of biddable pupils may worry about the student teacher's ability to cope in the local comprehensive schools, while a student who has failed to impress in an 'academic hothouse' may excel in a school which emphasizes the social and personal development of its pupils. Moreover, few teachers will have had experience of a broad range of schools to help them to locate their personal expectations within a wider set of standards. Prominent among teachers' concerns, therefore, are the needs for training and for standardization and moderation procedures to increase their confidence in their judgements.

Although mentors are acutely conscious that the performances they assess and their own judgements on these are context-specific, practice material and practical activities which would help them to calibrate their standards are not readily available. While it is an easy task to provide standardization material exemplifying different standards of performance in, say, a GCSE examination, the problems of doing this in the context of ITE are clear. It is a much simpler task to copy and disseminate a set of GCSE scripts than it is to capture and share a live, transient teaching performance. There are all sorts of practical difficulties entailed in more than one assessor sitting in on the same live performance. Alternatively, trying to create a permanent audio-visual record of a lesson has its own drawbacks. For instance, at any one time, a camera can capture only one aspect of a lesson while other features may be lost forever.

Finally, one should not overlook the distinctive nature of school-based training, for this also makes assessment a more difficult and delicate issue. First, much school-based training takes place on a one-to-one basis, making it a very personal form of training for both mentor and mentee. Secondly, many of the activities – self-assessment in which one explores individual strengths and weaknesses, counselling and support which follow a bad experience – can combine to make this an intimate, revelatory experience with the air of a confessional. Also, one should not forget the intensely personal nature of learning how to teach: 'a process in which people's whole sense of themselves is involved ... the experience of teaching, at all levels, is one in which our feelings, our sense of identity, our vulnerability as human beings are all involved' (Smith and Alred 1993: 106).

All of this compounds the level of personal involvement for the protagonists. No wonder, then, that teachers claim that mentoring works best when it is founded in a personal relationship in which there is mutual respect, trust and confidence. What are the implications for assessment of binding training into this type of close, personal relationship? A recent study which examined competence-based training in four different courses of higher education, including ITE, found that:

> Professional practitioners, especially those who had a sustained relationship with a trainee in the workplace, found it extremely difficult to combine the roles of support and assessment. External criteria for assessment helped in this, but in general assessors were reluctant to use them to 'fail' or not to pass someone whom they had come to regard as a working colleague ... In ITT teacher assessors ... feel that there is a discrepancy between their need to nurture and encourage students and their role as judge ... the judge is closer to the student who will live with the consequences of failure.
>
> (Bridges *et al.* 1995: 6 and 25)

One mentor reflected on her experience of binding assessment into such an intimate relationship as follows:

> Until very recently I was wholeheartedly in favour of the scheme but I do wonder if it is right to force such a deep relationship on people. Mentors who have had problems, sometimes resulting in Articled Teachers leaving the scheme, have all felt personally responsible and have suffered a great deal of anguish, a blow to their confidence and a loss of self-esteem ... I have recently suffered a minor set-back and can appreciate how devastating a 'failure' must be.
>
> (quoted in Jacques 1992: 345)

Assessment, especially summative assessment, requires a level of distance and objectivity which may be hard to attain when judgements have to be made in the context of 'involved' personal relationships.

Thus we should not underestimate the difficulties which are peculiar to this particular assessment task. Nevertheless, the basic requirements for the assessment of school-based ITE are the same as the basic requirements of any assessment procedure. Standard texts emphasize the need for an assessment to be valid (i.e. actually to measure what it purports to measure) and to be reliable (i.e. to produce results which are consistent and credible). An equally important requirement of any assessment system, which has been overlooked too often in the past, is the need for it to be manageable. The rest of this chapter considers ways of satisfying the criteria of validity, reliability and manageability within the context peculiar to school-based ITE, but first it is important to appreciate the context in which this work is undertaken.

The context for assessment

Much of the recent development, and the debate, surrounding the assessment of students' fitness for qualified teacher status has centred on a competence-based model of assessment. While competence-based approaches may be suitable for assessing preparedness for low-skill jobs, or those which focus on technical competence, their application to the professions has been a highly contentious issue, which has provoked vigorous exchanges between those who favour these approaches and those who see them as demeaning the special qualities and capacities required by the professions. As it is only possible to rehearse the arguments for and against briefly here, a fuller treatment of the issues can be found in Whitty and Willmott (1991), Berrill (1992), Furlong (1992), Pring (1992), Whitty (1992), Frost (1993) and Smith and Alred (1993).

Advocates of competence-based approaches claim that by specifying the outcomes which trainees must achieve, clear foci are provided for all those involved in the training process. This helps to ensure consistency of standards, providing a common training entitlement for all students regardless of where they are trained. Assessment is also made more rigorous. Competence-based frameworks reduce the subjectivity of the assessment, increasing employers' confidence in the credibility of the qualification. Students, too, have a clearer idea of the goals at which they are aiming. Critics see competence-based assessment as a narrowing and mechanical approach which focuses attention on behaviour and skills. The capacity to perform certain skills and behaviours is no guarantee of an intelligent understanding of the underlying knowledge and concepts which inform professional practice. The demonstration of routine competences which can be ticked off on a checklist is of little value if it is not informed by real knowledge and insight into how, why and when certain skills work. As well as knowledge and understanding, true professionalism is the embodiment of certain qualities, values and attitudes which narrow competence-based models neglect. Thus critics object to the atomization of professionalism, arguing that essential qualities are missed by such an approach. Not only is the professional person more than the sum of his or her parts, but it is also technically possible for an individual to satisfy the separate items on a list of competences while the total performance falls short of the standards expected of a professional person in that field.

Whatever one's standpoint in this debate, competence-based profiling has been enshrined in government policy on ITE by Circular 9/92 (DfE 1992). The circular lists twenty-seven teaching competences organized into five categories (for full details, see the Appendix):

- subject knowledge – three competences;
- subject application – seven competences;
- class management – four competences;
- assessment and recording of pupils' progress – five competences;
- further professional development – eight competences.

These, we are told, are to be the 'focus' for schools, higher education institutions (HEIs) and students 'throughout the whole period of initial training' and 'Their attainment at a level appropriate to newly qualified teachers should be the objective of every student taking a course of initial training' (Annex A). Although such pronouncements may sound rigidly prescriptive, Circular 9/92 does concede that the statements of the competences 'do not purport to provide a complete syllabus for initial teacher training' (p. 3) and that 'It is recognised that institutions are developing their own competence-based approaches to the assessment of students' (p. 4). Thus Circular 9/92 allows some discretion in the precise *content* of the training and the detail of the *assessment profile*, but the *form* which the assessment must take and its *basic constituents* are prescribed. The inspection criteria of the Office for Standards in Education (Ofsted 1993: 22) reinforce this prescriptive element by stating that, for the assessment of students' teaching competence to be judged satisfactory, there should be 'regular monitoring of the progressive development of the student's teaching competences in a profiling system jointly operated by the HEI and partnership schools'.

Since competence-based profiling appears to be here to stay, at least for the foreseeable future, some of those charged with the task of operationalizing the competences have taken advantage of the discretion built into Circular 9/92 and have challenged the notion that a competence-based approach is, by definition, incompatible with a more holistic approach to assessment, which incorporates professional capacities, values and qualities. Assessment schemes, such as those devised by Leeds University Secondary School Partnership (LUSSP) (Tomlinson 1995) and by the Open University for its recently launched part-time postgraduate certificate in education (Moon and Shelton Mayes 1995a, 1995b), have integrated a broad definition of the professional teacher into a competence-based profiling system. Only time and experience with these initiatives can determine their efficacy.

Principles for good practice

The components of the assessment

There are two basic components to the assessment process: *formative* and *summative*. Formative assessment is undertaken during the school attachment and places the accent on students' professional development. Its functions are two-fold. First, it provides *feedback* on past performances, thus helping students and mentors to identify strengths and weaknesses. As this statement implies, there is a *diagnostic* element to formative assessment, which helps mentors and mentees to analyse difficulties and to develop strategies for addressing them. Secondly, formative assessment has a *feedforward* function. The information provided by the feedback should inform future planning, determining the provision which the mentor makes for the student as well as influencing the student's preparation and classroom practice. Thus formative assessment is a dynamic process aimed at propelling students towards teaching competence. The evidence gained in this ongoing process contributes to the summative assessment, which is a more formal summing up of progress-to-date, which may occur at more than one point during the course – at the end of a school placement, for instance – and ultimately at the end of the course when pass/fail decisions have to be made.

Who should contribute to the assessment?

We have already pointed out that assessing students' teaching competence can be a daunting and isolating experience for mentors. Fortunately, it does not have to be like this. Assuming sole responsibility for judgements is bad assessment practice. By involving 'significant others' in the assessment, mentors not only improve their assessment practice by making their judgements more valid and reliable, but they also reduce their own feelings of anxiety. Sharing responsibility for assessment also helps to depersonalize the process. Significant others are those who have played a part in the student's professional development and their inclusion in the assessment process provides a more comprehensive picture of the student in different situations.

For a number of reasons, it is probably unwise for the student to teach only the subject mentor's classes and few mentors adopt this practice. As soon as a student assumes responsibility for another teacher's class, the teacher and the trainee inevitably become involved in a professional dialogue about the stage the group is at, topics already completed, what is likely to work with this class, etc. It is a short step from this kind of exchange to teachers becoming involved in students' professional development and ultimately in their assessment. Teachers in the mentoring department, therefore, have a logical contribution to make to the assessment of students' competence. However, the significant others extend beyond the members of the subject department. To gain a rounded and comprehensive picture of a student's total professional performance – that is, to improve the validity of the assessment – different aspects of the performance need to be taken into account: work in classrooms with different age and ability groups; work in departments beyond the student's own specialist subject; pastoral work including involvement with tutor groups and personal and social education; extracurricular activities; contributions to meetings, seminars and workshops, etc. Since no single teacher is likely to have experience of the student in all of these roles and settings, a comprehensive assessment of performance will involve gathering evidence and information from a range of sources. Those who have a role to play in the assessment process include:

- the subject mentor and the professional mentor;
- members of the department receiving the student;
- other teachers who have a professional involvement with the student;
- HEI tutors;
- the student, engaged in self-assessment;
- other students – where students are paired, there is the potential for formative peer assessment.

Involving a number of assessors also enhances the reliability of the assessment. The theory of assessment suggests that when judgements have to be made in areas which are subjective – as assessing teaching competence surely is – the reliability of the assessment can be improved by increasing the number of independent assessors who contribute to the assessment and the number and length of the occasions on which assessment is carried out (Gronlund 1985; Ebel and Frisbie 1991). In theory, the least reliable type of assessment entails a single assessor basing a judgement on a single, brief assessment event.

In a school setting, an assessment dialogue needs to be set up between all those who have a distinctive contribution to make. For instance, the subject mentor is likely to possess detailed knowledge about the classroom skills of a small number of students and that is the strength of his or her contribution. However, the subject mentor's knowledge and standards are likely to be bounded by the department. Professional mentors normally deal with larger groups of students and possess a wider perspective encompassing the whole school. Thus the professional mentor has an important role to play in broadening and coordinating the assessment of the individual student, and linking it to wider standards. This process is furthered by the HEI tutors. What the tutors lack in context-specific information about the particular school and the particular classes is compensated for by their breadth of experience of other schools and other students. Tutors have an important moderating role to play, calibrating standards in individual schools. The school's detailed situational knowledge is complemented by the tutor's wide-ranging experience. Thus each partner is able to contribute particular strengths and offset each other's weaknesses. Sharing the load has the added advantage of making the assessment more manageable. This gathering of a range of perspectives from different sources enhances assessment decisions. Nevertheless, responsibility for those decisions rests ultimately with mentors on most schemes.

Assessment criteria and processes

The criteria upon which the assessment will be based and the processes by which the assessment will be conducted should be fully documented, and disseminated to all those involved. The competences specified in Circular 9/92 (DfE 1992) must play a well-defined part in both the formative and summative assessment of the student. However, it is important to recognize that the competence statements were not presented as a straitjacket to contain either the course content or the assessment criteria. The way was left open for individual partnerships to develop assessment profiles which reflect the wider vision of professionalism embodied in their courses. (At the time of writing, a national Career Entry Profile is being trialled. If this is accepted or imposed, local profiling systems will have to take it into account.) To play their part effectively, all those involved in the assessment need to be in possession of this information. Students need an understanding of the goals at which they are aiming and the criteria against which they will be judged. Mentors, too, can only work in a focused, purposeful and consistent way on a partnership-wide basis if assessment criteria and processes are made explicit. The significant others who contribute to the assessment may undermine its consistency if they are ill-informed.

Although full and unambiguously worded assessment criteria are a prerequisite for good assessment practice, they alone cannot ensure that common standards are applied consistently. Differences in interpretation will arise and it is only by engaging the participants in an assessment dialogue, in which interpretations are shared and judgements are negotiated within and between schools and with HEI personnel, that assessors can hope to attain a professional consensus. The difficulties in ensuring that this becomes a part of one's assessment practice cannot be overestimated – not least finding the time to meet and collaborate in this way. Nevertheless, opportunities should be created wherever possible for joint assessment exercises involving teachers within and across schools and HEI tutors. Visiting moderators and external examiners also play a part in developing consistency of standards.

It is possible to construct very detailed and thorough assessment profiles consisting of large numbers of categories and sub-categories, each of which requires complex judgements to be made (e.g. a rating scale attached to each component). These fixed response scales may be supplemented by summary written comments. Such systems may appear impressive. However, it is important to recognize that unwieldy assessment profiles which require completion on several occasions may compromise the *manageability* of assessment. In this context, it is worth bearing in mind the findings of a piece of empirical research:

> Practitioners seemed to find it difficult in practice to assess trainees against more than about six significant criteria . . . In practice we found that teacher educators tended to reduce the lists of competences specified by the Department for Education to not more than six broad categories. This not only appeared to make assessment a more workable process but to go some way to accommodating their commitment to a holistic approach in assessing student teachers . . . Evidence shows that one of the consequences of the strain on teachers as resources decrease has been their 'unpreparedness as assessors' . . . In the cases studied it was the role of assessor rather than developer which appeared to suffer. Multiple duties can mean that there is not the time necessary to deliver the assessment system in the way which is intended . . . The assessment is then adapted to meet the practical constraints under which the assesor must operate.
>
> (Bridges *et al.* 1995: 6, 11 and 26)

This suggests a powerful case for making assessment procedures as simple and efficient to complete as possible without compromising the essential requirements.

Assessment in practice

In practice, assessment involves a range of activities:

- observing students engaged in classroom teaching and other professional activities;
- providing oral and written feedback on performance;
- facilitating students' self-assessment;
- monitoring the progress of individual students and making special provision for those who are experiencing difficulties;
- gathering evidence to document the assessment process and ensuring that copies of relevant materials are stored centrally;
- compiling interim and final reports on individual students;
- participating in training, standardization and moderation exercises;
- attending meetings/examination boards as appropriate.

In practice, some of these activities overlap; for example, a post-lesson tutorial is likely to include elements of student self-assessment and mentor feedback. However, for present purposes, it is sensible to try to deal with them separately as far as possible.

Observation

In this section, we consider observation specifically for the purposes of assessment. Traditionally, such observation has centred on students' subject-specific classroom practice and teaching skills. However, if assessment is to encompass the broader range of professional responsibilities, there is also a place for observing students in other contexts (e.g. working with tutor groups). Observation may take place on a formal or an informal basis. Courses lay down the minimum number of formal observations which mentors are required to make, whereas informal observations may take place as and when students and teachers deem them necessary. Formal observations should be spaced to allow students to demonstrate progress. Ideally, several informal observations should lead up to the first formal observation, which should not take place too early in the practice. As one professional mentor found, this requires careful forward-planning:

> Last year it was a real – I mean, I had, I can't remember the exact number of observations I had to do because we are contracted. I had like eighteen hours worth of observation to fit into a ten-week schedule and I made the mistake of thinking, 'Oh, no! You can't watch them at the beginning', so I gave them a couple of weeks to settle in and then, when I worked out the logistics, I thought, 'Oh no!' . . . It was a really close run thing.

As suggested in Chapter 4, it is useful to have key dates in an ITE reference file and on a year planner displayed in a prominent position. This can help in forward-planning and can provide a framework for when observations should take place.

It is good practice (in terms of validity) to vary the conditions of the observations – different teaching groups, different times of the day, different days of the week, different lesson types – to build a picture of the student in the full range of teaching situations. Observation can be particularly illuminating if a small number of foci have been identified in advance. So much happens during a lesson that too many foci or none at all may mean that the observation elucidates less than it might have done had it been more sharply focused. The process of identifying foci ties the observation into the students' experiential learning cycle of planning → implementing → reviewing, since the foci for a particular session are likely to have been identified during the action planning following a previous observation. As with all good teaching and learning, assessment is an integral part of the process. Observation is likely to be most productive and formative if the foci are negotiated with students and represent a genuine attempt to meet a shared perception of the students' needs. There is case study research which suggests that when trainers seek to impose their agenda on students, the mentoring has only a limited impact, with the students ignoring priorities that do not coincide with their own (Feiman-Nemser *et al.* 1993). The negotiation should also be informed by reference to the assessment criteria against which performances must be judged. A balance needs to be struck between addressing students' perceptions of their own needs and progressing towards the wider professional standards needed for qualified teacher status. However, the foci must not become a straitjacket constraining the observation. If other, perhaps unanticipated, aspects of the lesson are particularly important in determining its success or failure, these should also be noted.

There are other areas where careful briefing and negotiation beforehand can help to ensure that the observation runs smoothly and has productive outcomes. The following is a summary of the guidelines offered in Chapter 5:

- Has the lesson plan been seen and commented upon by the observer in advance?
- Is the observation formal or informal?
- What role, if any, will the regular teacher play in the lesson?
- How will the regular teacher react if pupils try to involve them in the lesson?
- Are there any conditions under which the observer should intervene in the lesson? If so, how are these to be signalled?
- Where should the observer be positioned?
- Which method, or combination of methods, of collecting data best fits the aims of the observation? For example, 'scripting' parts of the lesson to provide an objective, evidential record of the agreed foci; making diagnostic notes in response to the foci and other significant features of the lesson; time sampling predetermined categories of behaviour; interacting with pupils to gauge how far lesson objectives are being met. It may be that different phases of the lesson require different observation techniques.

Generally speaking, sessions, especially formal ones, should be of sufficient length to give a comprehensive picture of the activity under observation, which usually means a full lesson. There are occasions when observations might legitimately last for parts of a lesson; for example, if lesson beginnings or endings have been targeted for action, then the relevant section of the lesson could be observed. The value of dropping in on a lesson unannounced for a short while is questionable.

Verbal and written feedback

Observation of students should be followed up by verbal feedback. This will sometimes occur informally in the staffroom over a cup of coffee and, in other cases, a more formal post-observation tutorial will be arranged. Either way, verbal feedback should always be provided to allow for an exchange of perceptions and for the deepening of understanding which that exchange should promote. A dialogue may clarify misapprehensions and uncertainties which could arise from an exclusive reliance on written feedback. Written feedback provides a useful record, both for the student's own professional development profile/portfolio and for the school's assessment records. Over the course of the placement, the school should build up centrally held files of assessment evidence on each student to be used both formatively and in compiling final reports. There-fore, written feedback should always be provided for a formal obser-vation and for as many informal observations as possible. Try to ensure that the messages contained in the two types of feedback are consistent. The students in one empirical study reported feeling disconcerted when encouraging oral comments were at variance with harsher written criti-cisms (Tann 1994).

The timing of a post-observation tutorial is also important. Immediately after the lesson, the student may be in a state of emotional arousal which is not best suited to measured analysis and reflection. Therefore, if the assessor wishes to combine self-assessment with feedback, it is sensible to allow some time to elapse during which the student may reach a more objective judgement of the experience. If possible, the student should also produce a written evaluation so that the assessor and student may compare notes. However, if the time-lapse between observation and feed-back is too great, the value of the tutorial will be diminished. Just as pupils complain when teachers take a long time to mark their work that the for-mative worth of the assessment is devalued, so too for trainee teachers. Experiences which may have been extremely significant on the day when they occurred could have paled into insignificance several days later when the student has been overtaken by new and seemingly more pressing events. To maximize the learning potential of the tutorial, the feedback should ideally occur within twenty-four hours and certainly before the student teaches the class or the same material again. When scheduling observations, therefore, it is useful to think not only about the timing of the lesson but also how convenient the chosen lesson is for completing follow-up work. Where possible, these considerations should also be borne in mind when devising the student's teaching timetable.

Leading tutorials in a genuinely educative manner is a highly skilled activity. Common faults in conducting feedback sessions, which reduce their learning potential, include the following:

- the observer dominates the talk and provides insufficient opportunities for students to share and develop their own understanding;
- the observer sets targets for action rather than negotiating these with the student;
- the talk lacks a clear focus;
- the observer adopts the role of expert, assuming that their approach is the only or the best approach;
- the observer, in the role of expert, is too ready to tell the students what is wrong with their performance, rather than allowing the students to explore possibilities and progress at their own rate;
- the observer poses too many closed questions which elicit the answers they want to hear, rather than open-ended questions which lead to genuinely shared exploration and enquiry;
- the observer allows insufficient time for reflection which is, by its nature, a slow process;
- the observer, anxious to avoid undermining the student's confidence, is reluctant to criticize and offers only praise;
- the observer is insensitive (e.g. glances at watch or focuses exclusively on negative points);
- criticism is given in a destructive rather than a constructive fashion.

From this daunting list of pitfalls, one may conclude that skilled practice takes time to refine. Moreover, assessors are often oblivious to deficiencies in their own practice; for example, a teacher may be surprised to be told that they have dominated the talk! Therefore, it can be useful for mentors to sit in on each other's sessions or to view recorded tutorials as part of their own professional development. Some of the elements of good practice are implicit in the above list by way of contrast.

The tutorial needs to take place in a private venue where the participants are unlikely to be distracted by noise or intrusions. It is a good idea to invite the student to articulate their evaluation of the foci *first* as a way of opening the discussion. It is a basic educational principle that learning should start from the point that the learner is at. Allowing the student to open the tutorial gives the mentor access to that information and, as one mentor discovered, 'The tendency to talk at passive students is overwhelming at times. I learnt more when I listened.' There needs to be sufficient time to allow the discussion to develop before either of the participants has to leave or the room becomes unavailable. Asking focused but open-ended questions is a useful strategy for generating meaningful talk because, again, it puts the onus on the student to develop their understanding by articulating experiences. The observer can then add the points which they wish to make or challenge the student's interpretation of events. The student will also need time to read and reflect on the observer's feedback.

The tutorial needs to strike an appropriate balance between attention to positive and negative features, achievements and failings. Furlong and Maynard (1995: 84) highlight the criticism dilemma: students' fragile, emerging sense of professional worth can be crushed very easily even when criticism is sensitively handled. One of the aims of the tutorial must be to build students' confidence. Therefore, achievements must be recognized and recorded at an early stage in the proceedings. Equally, areas where improvement is needed must be addressed. The emphasis needs to be on constructive criticism provided in a positive way and the negotiation of strategies by which difficulties may be overcome. It is helpful if the student feels that support is being given in thinking the way forward, rather than an over-critical emphasis on the way things have gone. It is also helpful if students are encouraged to see teaching as a career-long process of professional development and learning, a rewarding and stimulating journey upon which the student is embarking – the observer is on the same journey, although at a more advanced stage.

Comments from students suggest that their experience of criticism may be very different from this. Too often, their perception of feedback is that they have been subjected to a barrage of criticism in which positive features have gone unacknowledged or have come so far down the list of criticisms that they have become too demoralized to 'hear'. Just as pupils cannot correct all of their faults at once and may be switched off by an over-emphasis on defects, so too in mentoring the priorities for immediate action need to be identified. Less pressing concerns will have to wait until later! No matter how sensitive and expert the mentor may be in handling feedback sessions, an unskilled member of staff may leave a student feeling bruised and inadequate. Not all teachers have the personal qualities and interpersonal skills to work with student teachers, and those who are considered suitable will need inducting into mentoring to ensure that they have been introduced to a repertoire of good practices. It is also essential to standardize certain practices to ensure consistency in the school's approach to assessment; for example, ensuring that everyone works with a common assessment pro-forma so that students are taken through the same processes by different observers, and ensuring that all assessments are copied to students and for centrally held records.

At the end of a formal post-observation tutorial, it is useful if the following have been achieved:

- a positive atmosphere in which progress and achievements have been identified and documented;
- targets which emerge out of a genuine negotiation have been established and recorded;
- provision which the mentor needs to make for the student has been agreed and recorded;

- actions which the student will take have been agreed and recorded;
- any negative feelings (anxiety, fear, confusion, resentment, etc.) have been aired and addressed as far as possible.

Student self-assessment

There are many reasons, both professional and procedural, why courses must make student self-assessment a formal feature. The role of self-assessment in supporting pupils' learning is now widely recognized. The importance of adult learners playing a proactive part in their own assessment is, perhaps, even greater (Gibbs and Habeshaw 1989). Many ITE courses promote a reflective practitioner approach (Schön 1983, 1991) to professional development and self-assessment is an integral part of reflective practice. Circular 9/92 (DfE 1992: Annex B) insists that courses should make 'specific arrangements for . . . formal opportunities for students to share their self-assessment with tutors and mentors'. The Ofsted (1993: 22) inspection criteria also state that, 'For the assessment procedures to be graded *very good* there will usually be . . . involvement of students in the identification of their progress and training needs'.

Consequently, most courses have developed some form of professional development record or portfolio, similar to a pupil's record of achievement, which students are responsible for compiling and which they take forward with them to job interviews and into their first teaching posts. By the end of the course, this should have developed into a comprehensive record of students' professional experiences and achievements, with different sections representing different aspects of the course. The items it is likely to incorporate include:

- the student's curriculum vitae;
- written reflection on developing personal and professional skills and qualities;
- summative assessment profiles and formal observation records;
- students' academic coursework and feedback comments;
- example lesson plans and associated evaluations; examples of pupils' work which has been assessed by the student.

At the Warwick Institute of Education, a record of professional achievement (ROPA) has been developed as part of the PGCE. It provides a focal point around which reflection and discussion of professional development needs and achievements may be organized. It is designed to be the vehicle for self-analysis throughout the PGCE year, with each student teacher taking personal responsibility for completing their own record. The ROPA uses a reflective questioning cycle based on the GRASP (Getting Results and Solving Problems) approach, which was originally developed as an approach to managing change and achieving results in an industrial setting. It has been adapted by the Comino Foundation for educational use in a number of Comino GRASP centres. [For a fuller description of GRASP and its use in educational settings, see Brooks and Little (1995) and Brooks *et al.* (1994).] The GRASP approach takes students through a questioning cycle which is intended to help them to do the following:

- formulate precise objectives;
- construct a clear picture of the results which they seek so that they know what the end-product will look like;
- explore alternative means of pursuing goals as a way of selecting the most appropriate;
- identify specific criteria by which performance may be judged;
- monitor progress on a regular basis and revise targets accordingly.

There is an input at regular intervals by tutors and mentors who can help students in various ways. Both have a useful role to play in target-setting. Students often set themselves targets which are unrealistic or over-ambitious for beginning teachers; alternatively, they may have difficulty in clarifying their goals. Identifying too many targets is also a common pitfall. When this happens, students may be overwhelmed by the enormity of the task and abandon it. Setting a small number of realistic goals is a useful antidote to student passivity, too, obliging those who are inclined to sit back and let the year take its course to accept ownership of parts of their learning and to take the initiative in furthering their own professional development. Teachers and mentors also have a role to play in helping students to identify performance indicators by which they may measure their own progress and in suggesting strategies which students might adopt in pursuit of their aims. Mentors and tutors are also useful at the review stage, acting as 'critical friends' by challenging students and offering alternative perspectives on progress.

The formal use of ROPAs, requiring the collation of evidence and written reflection, imposes a mental discipline on students which many find salutary:

> It's a focusing thing really. It makes you realize areas where you are lacking and it's something to refer to and follow up.
>
> (Student teacher)

> It's been good to have to write something down because it makes you think about what's going on.
>
> (Student teacher)

> It makes you think, 'What could I do?' If I didn't have it, I probably wouldn't do it at all.
>
> (Student teacher)

Mentors also find it a valuable means of structuring their work with students:

> Having a vehicle through which you can actually organize negotiating sessions – the ROPA has provided quite a nice focus for the activities which you are doing with the students: meeting with them every day to debrief them on lessons that they've taught, to discuss short-term targets for future lessons, to consider long-term objectives ... We've looked at other ways that they might have approached things, negotiating and evaluating performance.
>
> (Subject mentor)

At the end of the course, a summative statement is negotiated for students to take forward into their first teaching posts as a starting point for induction and further professional development. The aim here is to build continuity and progression into the transition from student teacher to newly qualified teacher. The ROPA is also intended to support the selection and recruitment process by improving the information available to potential employers.

It would be misleading, however, to suggest that student self-assessment in the context of ITE is an unqualified success and that there are no problems. Just as teachers who are required to act as developer and judge experience a conflict of roles, so too there may be a conflict of interests for students who are obliged to engage in self-assessment. Students, with one eye on their final qualification, may find it difficult to partake of the free and frank exchanges which self-assessment promotes with a person whose role will ultimately switch to that of judge. Thus there is an uneasy relationship between student self-assessment and summative assessment. Sometimes the distinction between the two is not drawn or is unsatisfactorily drawn in course procedures and documentation. This has been a problem in our experience with ROPAs. It is possible to delimit the two, presenting student records as the property of the individual concerned and guaranteeing confidentiality over the material in it. However, the distinction may appear an artificial one to students who will remain anxious about the use which may be made of information gleaned from their self-exposure in one-to-one tutorials. Thus the relationship between student self-assessment and the final judgement which has to be made remains an uneasy one. In essence, students are at the sharp end of the conflict between formative and summative assessment, developing and judging.

Students who experience serious difficulties

As discussed in Chapter 5, it is important to tackle potentially serious problems at an early stage and at a low level before they have had time to escalate. It is helpful if open relationships in which problems may be aired have been established. However, where there is a risk that a student may fail the course, clear, effective and prompt communication is especially important. This should involve all those who have a part to play in the student's professional development: trainer ↔ trainer and trainer ↔ trainee. In carrying out such a difficult and stressful task, the establishment of clear criteria at the pass/fail borderline which define when students are at risk of failing can support the process of passing judgement, as well as enabling the school to set precise written targets for the avoidance of failure. In reaching a final decision, the HEI should have an input – joint observation should be undertaken where possible. An external examiner will also usually visit such students.

Case study 1: Using the record of professional achievement – Michael's story

Michael, like other students we have met before him, failed to appreciate the value of the record of professional achievement [ROPA]. His reluctance to share this with us was the first indication that this aspect of the course was not receiving his usual high level of commitment. After several reminders, he admitted that he had only written a few aims for the school-based block practice and had disregarded the other sections, which invited him to think through the process by which those aims could be achieved. It became obvious that his reluctance was the effect of lack of understanding of target-setting. He had never been faced with goals, criteria of achievement and action planning. In this respect he was on a par with our pupils in pastoral sessions as they plan the road to improvement in their academic lives.

In response, we worked on a mock ROPA entry together:

What are you trying to achieve in this part of the course?

To become better acquainted with the National Curriculum.

How will you know when you have achieved your aims?

By the end of this part of the course I will have a working knowledge of the structure, terminology and specific contents of the attainment targets for my subject and will express this with confidence in discussions with other staff and in writing schemes of work and lesson plans.

How are you going to achieve your aims?

1 Focus on each attainment target separately.

2 For each attainment target:
   • read and question the statements of attainment;
   • refer to the department's schemes of work to see how the statement of attainment can be matched to practice;
   • build references to the statements of attainment in one week's lesson plans;
   • evaluate two different lesson plans or sets of work where the statements of attainment are more applicable.

3 Move to next attainment target.

Michael took advice and subsequently produced a detailed action plan in the ROPA booklet. We considered this to be an important development for Michael, since much of his professional life would need these skills of setting goals and determining a way to achieve them.

Case study 2: An ex-student's perspective on assessment – Jane's story

Towards the end of the second teaching practice, the daunting process of assessment takes place. Mental notes from education seminars are fading as the days get longer and you realize how quickly the year has passed. Groups of pupils are responding at last, even though it has taken some time to convince them of your dubious status as teacher rather than as student.

Assessment, we are told, will now take place in schools. It will take the form of observations and discussions involving mentors and other members of relevant departments and will be based on the CATE competences, established with a view to ensuring the development of a fully rounded teacher, but also instilling a sense of impending doom. The long list of criteria to fulfil includes all aspects of teaching from differentiation to time and classroom management. These can too easily be blown out of all proportion: they are simply a formalized representation of what you know already!

The benefits of having many people involved in your assessment are enormous: more voices of reassurance, more advice on difficult children and more available discussion time all help you to reach your own conclusions. Occasionally, however, personalities can clash and you may find yourself being observed by someone who is unaware of university practice or who will pick you up on things you may consider trivialities. Further, schools like to employ a member of the senior management team as a member of the observation team. This can feel daunting, especially as you may not know them well, although it is helpful to have an outsider's perspective. Things such as these underline the tremendous sensitivity that is called for in the mentoring process. We are human after all, and the individual nature of your assessor's and your own personality must blend to inform the final verdict on your professional capabilities. Negotiation is the key to a successful relationship with your assessors. An absence of judgemental language and an open mind can counteract feelings of being undermined and the inevitable lows that we all feel.

Observation styles will vary. Often, most useful is a blow-by-blow account of what you have said and done in a lesson. For a mentor to comment, 'You then said, "Be quiet and listen". What do you think about that?', is much more constructive than, 'This student uses negative language in lessons'. A thorough debrief should offer ample opportunities to discuss individual circumstances and comments. This is part of a good mentor–student relationship, which should contribute to the building of a full evaluative picture that includes the ability to be judiciously self-critical without sinking into a sea of judgemental pronouncements.

During lessons, the harshest critics are the pupils, and it is easy to dwell on an overheard 'Boring', or 'I hate this', especially last period in the afternoon. Nevertheless, pupils' observations are a useful way of highlighting areas for attention. However, post-observation feedback can often cause more consternation than the observations themselves or the pupils' comments. The space and time for this feedback is often difficult to organize, given the constraints on teachers' time. It is essential to set aside a period of time to discuss observation as close to the observation as possible; there is nothing worse than notes being read to you from an observation that took place several days before. This can cause defensive reactions or, worse, passive resignation, as you struggle to remember what it was you did! It is really helpful to formulate joint statements with the mentor, as writing these can help you to work through problem areas. I feel it is important for students to make clear how they felt about the experience – factors such as losing your lesson plan or failing to get the right photocopies ready in time could be assumed as your normal practice. Rather like a driving test, gaining feedback from observations requires a capacity for picking yourself up from minor setbacks and seeing the positives as well as the negatives.

The inclusion of third-parties in the assessment process can cause concern. Often, external examiners will visit during the practice to moderate the assessment procedure. This is one time when the school seems to be as nervous as you are! These external examiners, who from my experience are quite normal, kind people, can put both parties on edge. In my case, a rather vague 'phone call from the university about the visit of an external examiner put the cat among the pigeons: this was mainly due to lack of information about their role. Students 'phoned each other in the evenings with rumours that external examiners only visited those schools where one of the students was likely to fail. Last minute hysteria prevails as schools reflect upon the way that they have been assessing you and you wonder what you have done to deserve a dreaded visit.

With hindsight, it seems eminently sensible to have external examiners to oversee the process. It is probably the number of agencies involved and the inevitable bureaucracy which cause so much anxiety in the school.

Teachers are always being asked to prioritize and, when it comes to assessment, for students the priority is in building and sustaining a relationship with your school and your mentors which is conducive to sensitive negotiation. After all, the scheme is ultimately there for the student's support and development and to enable the student to play a positive role in the school – the experience should be one of mutual benefit and enrichment.

Case study 3: A student experiencing serious difficulties – a professional tutor's account

Pam was a mature student who embarked on a PGCE course when she was in her late forties. She had spent her career in industry but had always had a yearning to teach, which she had indulged by coaching the children of friends and family. When her employers announced a voluntary severance package to enable them to slim down their workforce, Pam, whose own family was now grown up, took the opportunity to fulfil her secret ambition. She was enormously dedicated to her goal and highly committed to the course, living in bed and breakfast accommodation on weekdays to allow her to follow the PGCE of her choice. Each aspect of the course was completed industriously and several hours of painstaking preparation went into each lesson which Pam taught. For some time, her mild manner, enthusiasm for teaching and conscientiousness obscured certain personal characteristics. Pam was mentally inflexible and was unable or unwilling to listen to her mentors' and tutors' advice and to act upon it. Nevertheless, she frequently declared her readiness to learn and avouched her belief that she was learning a lot from her trainers. Towards the end of her first school placement, Pam's subject mentor and the mentoring department were expressing increasing concern over Pam's failure to develop or to experiment with alternative practices both to the professional mentor and to Pam herself. In the final debriefing session, when the school's summative report was discussed with Pam, the professional mentor felt obliged to introduce the possibility of ultimate failure if Pam did not become less rigid in her approach and failed to heed the guidance of those responsible for her professional development. Pam was visibly shaken by the mention of the word 'failure', expressed some surprise at the judgements of the school, but nevertheless thanked the professional mentor for alerting her to their concerns and said she only wished that somebody had told her earlier. The professional mentor pointed out that the mentoring department had been trying to convey these points to her during their formative feedback. The professional tutor, who was aware of the difficulties and had indeed experienced them first-hand, tried to further explore and reinforce Pam's targets for her next school placement in a ROPA tutorial at the university at the end of the first school placement. Again, Pam displayed that idiosyncratic mix of qualities: soft speech, modest manner, apparent keenness to learn, coupled with the same mental rigidity which had characterized all previous exchanges and an inability to 'hear' what others said to her.

Pam's first school practice report was forwarded to her second placement school and discussions took place between the two professional mentors and the professional tutor. A decision was taken that it would be helpful to Pam if, as far as possible, she could make a fresh start in her new department unhampered by the reputation she had earned in the previous school. Thus, although the new subject mentor saw the summative report and suggested targets for future development, the full detail of what had happened at the first school was withheld. The professional mentor decided to monitor the situation closely but discretely in the early stages of the placement. However, a teacher from Pam's first department was acquainted with a member of the receiving department and so Pam's reputation preceded her anyway! During the second practice, the school clearly had some reservations about Pam's competence, but their views were expressed in cautious, qualified terms and signs of progress and improvement were emphasized throughout. The possibility of failure was not broached until a few days before the deadline for early warnings of possible failure, when the professional mentor contacted the professional tutor to say that Pam was progressing all the time and, of late, seemed especially receptive to the advice of others. Despite this, the school was unsure whether Pam had secured sufficient progress to take her above the pass/fail borderline. Additional visits by the professional tutor and subject tutor from the university were arranged hurriedly. However, due to the difficulty of finding a time when Pam was teaching which coincided with a time when tutors were free to visit the school, the visits were arranged for the second half of the following week.

When the professional tutor arrived at the school, she gradually became aware that Pam seemed ignorant of the reason for her presence and regarded a visit at this stage in the year as unwarranted meddling. Borderline cases will always be difficult to make a clear-cut judgement about. Nevertheless, the professional tutor had some serious reservations about the lessons which she observed, which were discussed with the professional mentor. The professional mentor explained that Pam had continued to progress since the tutor's visits had been arranged and that progress had been made in all of the areas about which the tutor was expressing reservations. Under pressure and made nervous by the tutor's visit, Pam had reverted to the bad, old habits which she was generally agreed by the school to be overcoming. The professional mentor felt that it would be wrong, therefore, to fail Pam on these grounds.

In the end, the judgement was made that Pam was on the pass side of the pass/fail borderline and a PGCE was awarded to her. Since schools do not recruit newly qualified teachers on the strength of qualifications alone, the function of Pam's references was to make clear the nature of the pass which she had secured.

BECOMING A MORE EFFECTIVE MENTOR

Introduction: What makes a 'good' mentor?

At a simplistic level, and ideally, school-based initial teacher education (ITE) is founded on the assumption that those selected to be mentors are 'effective' or 'good' teachers. Apart from the fact that some people become mentors by default or for purely pragmatic reasons, this view is existentially problematic because it takes it for granted that there is agreement on what it means to be an 'effective' and 'good' teacher. However, as Drake and Dart (1995) point out, when it comes to teacher performance, 'effectiveness', 'goodness' and even 'competence' are not, in themselves, standardized terms, because circumstances and contexts, as well as the philosophies and values of those making the assessment, are significant and influential. What this can mean in practice is illustrated by the following quotations:

> Sometimes it's difficult because you can see a student performing not very well and you know that in another school, with different kids and with different teachers they'd be alright, even good. Is it realistic to expect people to be good in all circumstances? I'm not sure any more. I'm afraid to say that, much as I disapprove of them on political grounds, I have suggested to students that they might like to think about teaching in the independent sector because you know that they'd get on fine there. Some people are more suited to academic type teaching and they do it well, but faced with a class that needs more in the way of control, they're useless.
>
> (Professional mentor)

> I did really well on my first practice and I thought I'd got it sussed. The teachers were pleased with me, they agreed with how I was trying to do things and I felt really comfortable there. But when I moved to my second school it was the opposite. I did things the same, I thought I was getting on well with the kids, but it turned out that

the teachers weren't at all impressed. And I couldn't understand it until my university tutor said, 'Look. It's not you. They have different values and ways of working there compared with at H'. But what got me was that I could have failed at that second place, doing what I was getting praised for at my first school.

(English student)

What constitutes a 'good' mentor is equally problematic. Much depends upon personal idiosyncrasies and the ways in which individuals are able to express themselves and be the sort of teacher they want to be within particular school contexts (cf. Nias 1989). Following on from this it would be an interesting and useful exercise to ask members of the mentoring team, individually and as a group, to reflect on what they believe would constitute enhanced effectiveness in their particular circumstances and then to identify strategies which might improve their effectiveness. If the team members agree that they want to develop certain mentoring skills (e.g. active listening), or to extend their repertoire of mentoring strategies, perhaps INSET time could be set aside for that purpose, or higher education institution (HEI) staff could be invited into school to run a workshop.

Having acknowledged that 'effectiveness' is subjective and contextual, it is the case that various commentators suggest that there are certain generally agreed characteristics and understandings that are shared by 'good' mentors and which can be developed. For instance, as noted earlier, interpersonal skills are extremely important and while some of these are to do with individual personalities, others can definitely be worked on and improved. In addition, being a 'good' mentor requires the 'acknowledgement by mentors that their own beliefs implicitly generate philosophies of teaching and learning in their subject' (Drake and Dart 1995: 124). Reaching this understanding may need some guidance of the kind that HEI staff are often well placed to provide, but again, this is an area which it is possible to develop. More generally, what is necessary is a commitment to taking an informed, critical, reflective and enquiring approach to all aspects of teaching, learning and schooling (cf. Furlong and Maynard 1995; Tomlinson 1995). In other words, a commitment to keep on learning. 'Good' mentors will, it seems reasonable to assume, hold this commitment and will want to become even better at their job. There is some evidence to indicate that in seeking to achieve this aim they are, at the same time, likely to become 'better' teachers:

Many teachers judge that they have benefitted professionally from their involvement in ITT [initial teacher training]. They have read more widely and thought more reflectively about their own practice in response to trainees' questions and HEI mentor training.

(HMI 1995: 2)

I have to say that since I've become a mentor I've probably become a better teacher too . . . I think, for me, it's because I've tried to be much more conscious about what I'm doing and why. I've felt that I should be able to justify things more and be able to discuss with the student why I did it that way and what the alternatives are. Over the years you tend to go on to automatic pilot and just do it. I don't mean that you're not always trying to do it better and you do evaluate and change your approach. You have to because each class is different and they respond to things in different ways, but I'm not sure that you really do it consciously, it's more a sort of reflex action really.

(Subject mentor)

Yes, it is more work, it's another thing but I think it's worth it. For me, at the moment, mentoring's just what I needed. I think it's forced me to take a step back and think about being a teacher. Things are so hectic in school, there's always so much to do and you get caught up in that but mentoring, while that's more paperwork in itself, it does bring you back to what it's all about, teaching kids in classrooms and finding the best way to do it. Would you believe I've even done some reading about teaching and learning styles and about equal opportunities! When the students were doing an assignment one of them had this book and I actually borrowed it and read most of it through. I didn't agree with it all but it did make me stop and think because it confirmed something I'd thought about the sexes having different learning styles and it gave suggestions for taking a fairer approach.

(Subject mentor)

In this chapter, we look at some suggestions for ways in which teachers generally and mentors in particular can work towards improving their practice through their involvement in school-based ITE. Rather than look at specific 'tips' for teachers (which cannot, in any case, be of general use, for such tips usually are context- or circumstance-specific), we advocate inquiry-based developmental approaches which can be adapted to meet the requirements of individuals and specific situations. Readers should note, and indeed it will become clear, that the line we take is based on a particular set of beliefs, values and assumptions; namely, that reflective, inquiry-based practice is synonymous with 'good' practice and, therefore, with 'effective' mentoring. Other writers might adopt quite a different approach.

Developing practice: A whole-school approach

Over the years many people, including such eminent figures as Lawrence Stenhouse, have criticized what seems to be the dominant attitude towards teacher development in this country, which is summed up in the way in which we talk about student teachers being on 'teaching *practice*'. Although there is a period of time in which entrants to the profession are described as 'newly qualified teachers' and, as such, are officially considered to be in need of extra support and guidance, attaining qualified teacher status means that they have been judged to be competent and are, by implication, no longer in need of 'practice'. Even using the competences of Circular 9/92 (DfE 1992) as a guide, such an assessment is somewhat problematic because (in the case of the majority of students) the judgements are made on the basis of performance in, at most, two schools and, as we have noted, contexts differ widely. Previously, as most readers will recall, the first year of teaching was an assessed 'probationary year' which had to be passed before qualified teacher status was confirmed. Now there is not even that and it seems to us that being a newly qualified teacher carries quite a different meaning and far more in the way of status and identity as a teacher than being a 'probationer' did.

The situation with regard to teacher development is not quite as straightforward as such a simplistic linguistic analysis might suggest. As professionals, many (if not most) teachers are concerned to develop and improve their practice and to gain a wider understanding of the various issues and areas which impinge upon their work. Furthermore, since the mid-1980s, all teachers have been obliged to attend in-service training sessions. On the face of things, and in reality, greater numbers of teachers than ever before are actively involved in professional development of one kind or another. School-based ITE generally, and the experience of being a mentor in particular, have the potential to extend and enhance the personal and professional development of teachers even further and can, if approached and conceptualized appropriately, offer many opportunities for in-service education.

As noted earlier, schools become involved in ITE mentoring programmes for a variety of reasons. Some do so because they see it as offering the opportunity to build or consolidate an existing school culture in which the emphasis is on continuous and continuing teacher development. Research into 'effective schools' (e.g. Riddell and Brown 1991) indicates that such an emphasis contributes to the creation of a strong and positive ethos and to a 'good' learning environment for pupils, as well as for teachers and student teachers. Mentoring can, therefore, be beneficial for the whole school population (Shaw 1992: 82).

Where the culture of the school does place a premium on teacher development, the following will be found:

- strong support from senior management;
- being a mentor will be seen as making a definite and positive contribution to developing and enhancing teacher skills and knowledge;

- teacher education needs will have priority in the school development plan;
- there will be policies concerned with all aspects of teacher education;
- there will be realistic time and resource allocations for ITE and INSET activities;
- teachers will see and be encouraged to see their classrooms and the school as a 'source for professional development' (Thiessen 1992: 86);
- there will be open and continuing debate about what constitutes effective teaching and learning and about what needs to be provided, in the way of training, for this to be achieved;
- all teachers, no matter how experienced they are, or whether or not they are mentors, will be expected, as a matter of course, to research and reflect on their practice and to question the assumptions, beliefs, values and philosophies which underlie it.

In short, there will be a whole-school commitment to improvement through teacher education.

An inquiry-based approach to mentoring

Inevitably, given the overwhelming demands made on schools and teachers, these requirements sound time-consuming and idealistic in the extreme. What is being suggested, however, is injecting a degree of rigour and system into what many teachers already do intuitively and as part of their everyday practice. Whether they do so consciously or not, many teachers do take an inquiry- or action-research-based approach to their work. As one mentor said, teachers reflect upon what they do and how they do it in the light of how their pupils respond and make modifications or more substantial changes on the basis of those reflections. Alexander (1984) advises that 'learning to teach must be a continual process of hypothesis testing' and it is difficult to see how it can be anything else. For even if teachers eschew formal theory, their practice is, nevertheless, based on their own experientially founded theories. Like others (e.g. Stenhouse 1975; Elliott 1990; Husbands 1995c), we are proposing that teachers should take an explicitly research-based and reflective approach to their work and should adopt a 'conceptualization of professional development as grounded in systematic workplace inquiry' (Husbands 1995c: 21). If mentors take such an approach to their own teaching, they will have an enhanced understanding of their personal theories, they will be in a better position to begin to articulate their tacit and taken-for-granted professional knowledge, and they will be more aware of the contextual variables that have such a significant impact upon all teacher–pupil encounters. In short, by seeking to understand their own professional

practice, they should be in a better position to help other people understand theirs. Also of considerable importance is the model that they will
be presenting to the student teachers they work with, for the evidence suggests that student teachers do adopt 'the culture and practices of the school
and of the teachers with whom [*they*] have contact' (Williams 1993: 409).
Thus, if students see practising teachers taking a reflective, research-based
approach, then they will be less inclined to dismiss it as an unrealistic
notion of academics. Husbands (1995c: 23) notes that 'a view of teaching
as research-based, reflective activity makes any effective distinction
between [*theory and practice*] impossible'. In the quest for effective teaching and learning (whether that be by students, teachers or pupils), there
is no distinction between theory and practice either.

So how can teachers begin to take a systematic research-based approach
to their work? The HEI that the school is working with is the first and
obvious place to start. Many HEI–school partnership programmes involve
an element of in-service provision or reduced fees on higher degree
courses as part of their financial agreement. Indeed, a number of mentors
have taken advantage of such arrangements and enrolled on courses to
pursue simultaneously their mentoring enquiries and improve their
qualifications. Even where such agreements do not exist, it is usually possible to negotiate with the HEI for specific input. There are almost certainly
bound to be lecturers at the HEI who are interested or involved in 'teacher
as action-researcher' work and who would welcome the opportunity to
collaborate or provide some guidance. Even nearer to home, in many
school staffs there will be someone who has, by one means or another –
often on a higher degree course – been introduced to the approach and
who is willing to share their knowledge and expertise. All too often people
go on such courses and have little opportunity to put what they take away
to any use; this is an ideal chance for them to do so.

There are also many books on the subject. 'Classic' texts include:

Elliott, J. (1990) *Action Research for Educational Change*. Milton Keynes:
   Open University Press.
Hopkins, D. (1985) *A Teacher's Guide to Classroom Research*. Milton Keynes:
   Open University Press.
Stenhouse, L. (1975) *An Introduction to Curriculum Research and Develop-
   ment*. London: Heinemann.

What teachers decide to research will depend upon their own interests
and concerns and, perhaps, upon their school's development plans.
However, given that mentors are concerned to become more effective in
that role, they may, initially, choose either to look at aspects of mentoring
or to work on similar areas to those that the students are focusing on. For
instance, if a student is working on his or her questioning technique, then
so can the mentor. The value of doing it in this way is two-fold. First, it

enables the mentor to share at first hand in the student's experience. This can result in valuable insights into what the mentoring programme might 'feel like' to participants. Secondly, it requires them to bring their own professional and contextual knowledge to bear upon the situation. This may help them to better guide and advise the student who does not have such knowledge to draw upon. Having said this, mentors should be sufficiently open-minded to learn from the student should the opportunity arise.

Probably the most appropriate and convenient way of building in an action research approach is through the focused observations that will already be part of the mentoring programme. When students observe teachers, the emphasis is on what the student can learn. An equally useful approach is to present observation in terms of a research and learning opportunity for both parties. Depending upon the student's experience and the teacher's interest, teacher and student can work together in deciding:

- what the focus of the observation should be;
- how the observation should be conducted;
- how 'data' should be recorded.

The feedback session can then be a collaborative learning affair, with the teacher having the rare opportunity to reflect on what the student has observed and to bring their experience and knowledge to the analysis of their performance.

> I have found the feedback sessions following students observing me to be extremely valuable. You don't often get the opportunity to see yourself, as it were, and you can learn an awful lot. In our department we've tried to make use of having the students in to improve our own teaching. If you focus their observations and tell them precisely what you want them to look out for, then you can take a systematic approach and people feel less threatened . . . It was a bit odd at first and some people weren't entirely happy with it because they felt vulnerable and afraid that the students were passing judgement. That's why we've gone for precise observation schedules. We specify exactly what sorts of behaviours they are to focus on and try and keep the reporting objective, and once people have got used to it they've found it really helpful. We did try it out amongst ourselves first and that was good. I also think it's a good idea to be on the receiving end of what you're doing to the students. If you know what it feels like, then you think a bit more carefully about how you give feedback, how you ask questions, because you're more conscious of how sensitive you can feel and how an innocent comment can really upset you.
>
> (Subject mentor)

The teacher quoted above mentioned that she and her colleagues, as